D1600824

MAKING MONEY

MAKING MONEY

by
Ian Andersen

**THE
VANGUARD PRESS**
New York

Have more than thou showest,
Speak less than thou knowest,
Lend less than thou owest.

—KING LEAR

SHAKESPEARE

CONTENTS

7

MAKING
MONEY

INTRODUCTION

● Much has been written about cutthroat business. It often seems that capitalism has become inextricably intertwined with "putting the other guy down." "Profit can be obtained only at another's expense." Some time ago, it occurred to me that this thesis ain't necessarily so. Why must I step on someone else to reach monetary goals? In fact, it seems counterproductive to fill my need for money in this fashion. Usurping another's power does not produce wealth, it produces enemies. And enemies can turn on you. So beware! I find I must keep my ambitions absolutely clear. Is it money I seek, or power? Do I need to elevate my ego or my net worth? Do I merely want to get rich, or must I *beat* someone? Ten years ago I realized that my business needs were exclusively fiduciary in nature. Ego and power needs could be filled elsewhere.

In America we are programmed to playing win-lose games. A weekend football game typifies this brain-washing. The victors are elated, the losers humiliated. Children, especially male children, are imbued with this philosophy throughout the developmental years. (If you disbelieve, watch a few TV ads for kids' toys.) Secondary school is replete with competition — sports, grades, clubs, honor rolls, societies. College and gradu-ate school reward one-upmanship. Slipping in that little-known fact at just the right time, as when a fellow classmate is floundering, reaps rave reviews from professors. This win-lose behavior, so generously rewarded throughout the formative years, is carried over into business. It provides the framework for money-making activities. But this philosophy has its consequences. By stepping on others you set yourself up to be stepped on. Leaving enmity and animosity in your wake inevitably creates jeopardy. They're out to get you! And with good reason.

I have been enormously successful at making money. What turns me on is playing games where others make the rules. I like to study all the parameters and systematically approach the problem of how to win — and keep winning. Two components must be considered. The first is to understand money-making games and apply a winning system. The second is the psychology of perceiving the behavior and needs of the other players. The secret of making money is to integrate these two components.

When this principle is properly applied, there are no losers. Everyone wins! Of course, this concept is not applicable to all areas of making money, but it can be applied, at least in part, to a surprisingly large number of potential investment fields — stocks, real estate, cashflow management, credit, interest, insurance, commodities, and precious metals. Once money is made, how, then, do you keep it? This is addressed in chapters on income taxes, Swiss banks, Liechtenstein corporations, inflation hedges, tax havens, and foreign currencies.

I

Negotiating:
How to Deal with People

1. The Art of Negotiating

"You can generally get success
if you do not want victory."
WILLIAM RALPH INGE

● How can we get what we
want in life? This is a basic issue for us all. The answer
is "Through negotiation." Whether it's feeding ourselves, obtaining recognition from our peers, or getting
that "hot date" into bed, the answer to the fulfillment of
many needs is negotiation.

Negotiating is an art — a learned skill. But when
and where do we learn these essential techniques? Certainly not in school. Precious few institutions, including
those of higher learning, offer courses in negotiation. So
we are forced to learn from the "school of hard knocks"
how best to achieve the ends we seek.

Oftentimes reality is not what we would like it to

be. I recently read an ad from an institution for behavior modification: "Come in and tell us your goal and we will teach you how to achieve it."

Curiosity got the best of me, so I called. I was referred to an articulate woman who bluntly told me that, for a price, their group would create a programmed learning course to enable anyone to achieve a specific end: "Say you have a child in high school who needs high grades to go to college. He might work extremely hard and get nowhere. What we teach, if grades (not knowledge) are the object, is 'intellectual charm.' He will be taught classroom demeanor, the appearance of attentiveness, effective communication with the teacher, and the use of body language and facial expressions to convey interest and receptiveness (like smiling a lot at the teacher). He will be thoroughly drilled in how to ask questions to which he already knows the answers, and how to add to the teacher's response, repeatedly demonstrating what a quick study he is. In six weeks we can program him to be so charming, disarming, and convincing that we *guarantee A's or your money back!*" Incredible!

Kind of gets your goat, doesn't it? To think that a child can be trained to get good grades solely by his behavior is somehow appalling. Yet, if you put conventional morality aside for a moment (which I've learned to do more and more easily), you can see her point. She guaranteed nothing about knowledge, only grades. I've learned from experience that grades at all levels of education are a function of effective interaction with teachers. It's not what a child knows, but what the teacher perceives that counts. Remembering facts is secondary to *using* those facts one remembers. It's not surprising that this institute guarantees its results. It is dealing with *reality*. It provides a child with the necessary tools to fill a specific need — the desire for good grades. You may not like it, but that's how things are in the world of education.

Business revolves around money and power. Pure and simple. Who has the upper hand? Who needs whom the most? The guy in the driver's seat sticks it to the other guy. When the tables are turned and we find ourselves in a position of relative weakness, we are taught to be suppliant, bending to the will of the whip hand. By showing proper deference we may be thrown a bone. This "topdog — underdog" relationship is the *modus operandi* in the business world. One side wins, the other loses. Then conditions often change and positions on the seesaw are reversed.

Although power and intimidation are reality in business, their use as negotiating tools have very real consequences. Fear and guilt become the primary motivators for action. And they breed hatred and resentment. Intimidation may work for a while, but your victims will be gunning for you, snatching the first opportunity for revenge. This positioning often leads to the downfall of conquerors. As soon as a faster gun comes along it's curtains for the once mighty. Few tears are shed when a business despot gets his comeuppance.

Many studies have shown that reward is a stronger motivator than punishment. One study dealt with two groups of hungry rats. The object was to compare reward and punishment as motivators. The rats were placed in a maze. One group was given an electric shock each time they chose the *wrong* way. The other group was given food each time they chose the *right* way. The group rewarded by the food found its way through the maze significantly faster than the group motivated by punishment.

Fear and guilt are forms of punishment. These negotiating weapons may get the job done for now, but results are likely to be short-lived and fraught with consequences for the future. Based upon reward being a stronger motivator than punishment, I have tried to structure my negotiations around mutual-need fulfillment. I don't look at negotiations as battles where I either win or am vanquished. To me, negotiating is the dynamic process of need fulfillment, and the more aware I am of the needs of those I deal with, the greater my chances of success. In a successful negotiation *everyone* wins. When everybody wins, all parties are happy and this paves the way for future dealings. I have not had to pay more for being considerate of the needs of others — quite the contrary. I have found the negotiations that resulted in the greatest monetary returns have been those in which I was most tuned in to the needs of the other participants. Often, needs may not be pecuniary. Ego, status, and companionship needs are common. Interaction at this level is usually avoided in business dealings. I think they are quintessential! I have found that, when I elevate business relations beyond mere dollars and cents, I form a strong foundation for future activities. Instead of trying to scare others into doing things my way or suffering the consequences, I go out of my way to make sure all parties are comfortable. If I even sense that someone's nose is out of joint, I make every effort to ferret out his grievance. Experience has taught me that dissatisfied parties can be a nuisance, and that a trivial misunderstanding can snowball into a "cause célèbre." Once out on the table, negative feelings can be dealt with and resolved, but, pent up inside, they can fester and spread, feeding the paranoia that many harbor in dealings involving money.

MUTUAL-NEED FULFILLMENT

To be a good negotiator you must be a good listener. Before you can fill the needs of others you must perceive the nature of their needs. Needs fall into two basic categories — tangible and intangible. Tangible needs are food, shelter, safety, and sex. Intangible needs include ego, power, status, compassion, and self-actualization (maximizing your potential as a human being).

Not long ago I wanted to buy a specially situated lot on the beach in Hawaii. The lot was not on the market and was owned by a wealthy widow. I contacted some knowledgeable realtors who told me they had presented several very reasonable offers, but the property was not for sale. The owner didn't need the money and loved the property. Next, I tried to find out as much about the owner as I could. I discovered that she was about fifty years old, very bright, and a tough businesswoman. She tended to be a loner. She had tons of money and had one of the finest collections of art and antiques on the island. She specialized in art nouveau.

One thing about having gone to grad school is you learn how to become an "expert" in a subject overnight. A couple of days at the library and I was ready to pay the lady a visit. I phoned her, identifying myself as a business consultant from the mainland. I told her I was in Hawaii on business and had heard she had an exceptionally fine art-nouveau collection. I told her I had just begun collecting and very much wanted to see her collection to get a few tips from a true connoisseur. I said I really needed her help, because I had already made a few costly mistakes. She was quite cordial on the phone and invited me over that afternoon.

It was not difficult to be enthusiastic about her collection. Her house was like a museum, filled with exquisite lamps, furniture, trappings, and artwork, tastefully displayed and illuminated. My crash course paid off: I recognized the Daum lamps and the barber's-pole style of the British pieces, ogling appropriately. I complimented her on her taste and asked pertinent questions about how to acquire such pieces, costs, availability, et cetera — questions designed to be insightful and perceptive. (Note the close comparison to getting good grades!) She was delighted with how quickly I tracked the conversation, grasping the really pithy stuff, while glossing over the chitchat. I could tell that she liked me. She was glowing.

I asked if I might see the gardens. I had noticed a beautifully choreographed mélange of colors on my way in, and plants are something I happen genuinely to know something about. We discussed flowers for a while and I dropped a few pearls from my experience that excited her. I described in detail the loveliness of a native, fragrant California azalea (one of her favorite kinds of plants), and told her I would arrange to have some sent to her.

By the time we returned to the house we were both beaming. I thoroughly enjoyed this cultured lady, and she felt completely at ease. When we returned to the house, she asked the nature of my business. I said I represented a number of clients, and did international financial consulting. I was in Hawaii evaluating land investments for my clients, but had been so won over by the surroundings that, if I could find just the right piece of land, I would build a house and spend a major portion of my time in the islands.

The bait was out and she nibbled at it. She told me she had been quite successful in her real-estate investments in Hawaii, and currently owned a number of properties. I set the hook. I described exactly what I was looking for, a description that bore an amazing similarity to the particular lot I knew she owned. Suddenly her face lit up. "Why, I own a lot that might fit your needs very well. I hadn't planned on selling it, but we might work something out," she mused.

I acted duly surprised and *was* genuinely enthusiastic. She drove me out to the property and I fell in love with it before her very eyes. "This is one of the most beautiful homesites I have ever seen," I said, gazing out over the shimmering Pacific. "Would you really sell it?"

"I know you will appreciate this property and that it will be tastefully used," she said. "That would make me happy. Besides, maybe you could give me some business advice."

I responded with alacrity, assuring her that I would give her whatever advice I could. I asked her how much she wanted for the property. She gave me a price *lower* than the amount I knew she had been of-fered in the past. (I had found out the amounts of pre-vious offers from the realtors.) I accepted. I now have a lovely home in Hawaii, a new business client, and a very close friend and adviser in art-nouveau antiques (which I currently collect for real). Not too shabby!

Let's take a look at the mechanics of this negotia-tion. This fine lady had low monetary needs. She had strong ego, status, and companionship needs. Finding someone who shared her interests and appreciated her tastes pleased her greatly. So much of her being was invested in cultivating her refinements, that *recognition* of her accomplishments and esthetics made her feel good about herself and the energies she had expended. In some part she attributed this sense of well-being to my presence, so she naturally was inclined to help me fill my needs (in this case the acquisition of her choice lot). I'm sure at some level she wanted to have me around, so providing me with a lot so close to her home assured a continuing connection. Everyone won! We both got what we wanted and are still getting what we want from each other. She is less lonely, having made a fast friend, and is more comfortable with her invest-ments. Her ego needs continue to be met as she continues my education in art nouveau (she has a wealth of knowledge in the field), and her self-actualization needs are likewise being met as I have kindled an interest in botanical gardens and international finance, which she now eagerly pursues. For my part, besides the home-site, some of my monetary needs are being filled (a new substantial client), and my self-actualization needs are also being fed by my newly acquired interest in art nouveau. As a bonus, I have a new friend whom I admire and respect. A perfect negotiation!

A negotiation like this is very pleasant, with desirable long-term consequences. We both took an immediate liking to each other. That made things easy. But you don't have to be crazy about the person you are dealing with. More often than not, you may actually dislike someone you need. No matter. As long as you accurately perceive his needs, and he has the power to fulfill yours, the marriage is made. Remember, you don't have to live with your new bride twenty-four hours a day.

Not long ago I was playing blackjack at a large club in Reno. Blackjack is a lucrative game if you know how to count the cards and not get thrown out.* I was winning steadily, but the not-getting-thrown-out part was beginning to worry me. The casino manager, a sour cuss in his early sixties, was hawking me. The guy never seemed to sleep. Be it four in the morning or four in the afternoon, he would pop up whenever I made a play. After ducking and dodging for a couple of days, I decided I'd better talk with this old duffer. You see, I

* For a complete description of how to do this, read *Turning the Tables on Las Vegas* by Ian Andersen, Vanguard Press, 1976.

had a need to fill — I wanted to continue playing. He had the power to stop me. Despite my strong feelings of repulsion, I entered a negotiation. I invited him to have a drink, and he accepted. At first he was distant and prodded me to tell him about my twenty-one abilities (*his* purpose in having the meeting). But before long I steered the discussion away from blackjack and onto safer turf. The conversation meandered for a while, then suddenly I struck a nerve — fishing! His passion! His eyes lit up as he started rambling on about his exploits — "Two weeks ago, I caught a five-pound bass," he boasted.

"A five-pounder," I said. "Unbelievable! What did you use for bait?"

"Water doggies," he replied. "Best damn bait there is for bass."

Can you believe it? Water doggies! Hearing it from the mouth of old sour puss was *really* funny. Not that I had the foggiest idea of what a water doggy was. Nor did I laugh! The conversation continued for a full forty-five minutes before he was called away — he the teacher, I the willing neophyte. Right! His ego needs were being filled. Plot sound familiar? Then I set off to do some discreet detective work.

Within an hour I unearthed the definition of a water doggy. It's a type of newt that bass seem to have a craving for. Fascinating! Two more hours and I had one hundred of the critters in a tidy package. I put them next to me at the blackjack table and started playing. Within minutes my ubiquitous host appeared. Before he could say anything, I presented him with the gift I had prepared (filling his recognition and status needs). He was touched. He invited me to go fishing with him and I readily agreed, although we didn't firm up a date. Now, a year later, I still have no problems playing at this casino. We still talk fishing and we are still filling each other's needs. Strike a blow for water-dog power!

This philosophy may stick in your craw. Yet the inescapable fact is that *mutual needs are being fulfilled.* Sure, a good part of it is an act, a game, but a win-win game. When both parties feel good about a point in question, everyone wins! I can harvest life's goodies and make people happy in the process. What could be better?

I'll tell you what would be better. I'd like to be able to go up to someone, state my desires straight out, and have them filled. If I can help that person, I would gladly return the favor. Let's see how this approach would have worked with the woman who owned the lot I wanted in Hawaii. . . . I prance up to her door and say, "I understand you are the owner of a prize lot on the beach. I know others have made offers and that you have turned them down. Nonetheless, I would like to buy your lot. I know money doesn't mean that much to you, so I am willing to give you companionship, recognition, and respect. I know quite a lot about plants and I will share this knowledge with you. I understand you are pretty well heeled. I'm clever with money and (for a fee) will gladly give you the benefit of my advice. In time, I think we'll really get to like each other, as we seem to share mutual interests. In addition, I will give you a fair price for your choice lot."

That done, I immediately hop on a plane to Reno. I go right up to old sourpuss and say, "I'm an expert blackjack player. I know you have a responsibility to protect the casino, but I need the money. In exchange for letting me go on winning unmolested, I will satisfy some of your ego and status needs. We can talk about fishing, for example. To show that my heart's in the right place, I'll go out and buy you a hundred water doggies tomorrow."

How's it sound so far?

This type of approach reminds me of the peasant who, by a well, meets a maiden he finds particularly attractive. Not knowing how to make contact, but wanting the woman, he asks his friend, more knowledgeable in such affairs, how to approach the situation. His friend tells him to paint one leg of his horse yellow and ride by the maiden. "She's sure to notice you then."

Next day the peasant takes his friend's advice, paints one of his horse's legs yellow, and rides by the maiden. Alas, she doesn't even look up. He goes back to his friend and relates his sad experience.

"Paint all the horse's legs yellow," his friend suggests.

Next day the peasant gallops by the maiden with his yellow-legged horse. Again the maiden continues with her chores, without seeming to notice him. Dejected, he returns to his friend.

"Paint the whole horse yellow," his friend urges.

He does so, and next day rides right up to the maiden. Startled, she looks up and says, "Look, a solid yellow horse!"

Elated at being noticed at last, the peasant says, "Yeah, let's screw!"

Direct, but ineffectual. It just won't get the job done. I'm much more pragmatic. I try to choose the course of action with the highest probability of success. This often involves dealing with sensitive, intimate subjects — ego, status, companionship — and I just can't come galloping up on a solid yellow horse, unfurl a document that looks like the Magna Carta, and read off what I'm going to do. It's much more effective to ease into things. First, I must ingratiate myself to the people with whom I'm dealing. I find a topic of conversation that interests them, one in which they feel safe. Then, on more solid footing, they tend to open up. I tune in to what they are saying. The more comfortable they become, the more likely they are to share their needs with me. If I'm patient and listen actively, they will make their needs known. I don't have to call their attention to these wants; I just have to fill them. The basis for negotiation has been established.

CHARACTERISTICS OF A GOOD NEGOTIATOR

Table I lists the characteristics of a good negotiator. The ambience surrounding a negotiation is fundamental for success. This point cannot be stressed too strongly! If you go into a parlay with a chip on your shoulder (the "I'll show that sonofabitch" philosophy), you minimize your chances of getting what you seek.

The ideal negotiator sets a cooperative climate. He is ingratiating and attentive. He listens carefully, perceiving the total message being communicated (both

TABLE I

CHARACTERISTICS OF A
SUCCESSFUL
NEGOTIATOR

1. Ingratiating
2. Respectful
3. Supportive
4. Considerate
5. Confident
6. Caring
7. Empathic
8. Attentive
9. Perceptive
10. Competent
11. Patient
12. Creative
13. Open-minded
14. Flexible
15. Charming
16. Controlled
17. Temperate
18. Soothing
19. Modest
20. Thorough
21. Trustworthy
22. Good listener
23. Assertive

TABLE II

ATTITUDES OF AN
UNSUCCESSFUL
NEGOTIATOR

1. Hostile
2. Argumentative
3. Defensive
4. Inconsiderate
5. Intimidating
6. Attacking
7. Angry
8. Unresponsive
9. Indifferent
10. Dogmatic
11. Distant
12. Insensitive
13. Threatening
14. Overbearing
15. Belligerent, pressuring
16. Domineering
17. Disrespectful
18. Opinionated
19. Suspicious
20. Guarded
21. Confusing
22. Poor listener

nonverbal and verbal). He is patient, open-minded, and modest. When dealing with this ideal negotiator, you get a feeling of trust and support. He comes off as competent and thorough, yet creative, directing problem-solving toward mutual-need fulfillment. His power comes through having developed his human potential, a development that commands the respect of others. He is confident, but not arrogant; centered, but flexible; controlled, but not intimidating. In a nutshell, he's a guy that makes you feel good about yourself! You like him, trust him, and want to be associated with him. You admire his knowledge and abilities, yet feel he is tuned in to your needs and cares about you.

The good negotiator is in touch with his own emotions and aware of his weaknesses. He is not afraid to admit when he is wrong, and not afraid to say, "I don't know." Far from superhuman, he is effective because he is *so human*. He is strong because he is secure enough to confront his drawbacks and share his feelings with others, rather than attempting to cover a basically insecure emotional framework with a veneer of aggressive, hard-driving strength.

ATTITUDES OF AN UNSUCCESSFUL NEGOTIATOR

Table II summarizes traits to be avoided in negotiations. You will recognize many of them. They are the stock in trade of the typical business negotiation. The emotion at the root of many of these characteristics is fear. As Shakespeare said, "In time we hate that which we often fear." Over the longer term, fear-oriented relationships break down. These arrangements are held together by a fine thread. Eventually that thread snaps. Such negotiations are ineffective, the results partial at best, the relationships short-lived.

Negotiation is an ongoing process — as dynamic as life itself. As long as human beings interrelate, they will negotiate. This is the main reason why negotiations based on fear break down. As long as the two parties remain in contact, the negotiation continues and the wheel turns. Results based on fear are win-lose games and, at first opportunity, the losing side will try to gain the upper hand. Far better is a result where both sides perceive they have gained from the interaction and *want* to continue the relationship.

Negativism can creep into negotiations, poisoning a cooperative, problem-solving atmosphere. At times I have been so totally engrossed in a project that I have been unaware of changes in climate. Tension, suspicion, defensiveness, or fear may slip in quite unnoticeably. In retrospect, there were warning signs that I was not sharp enough to pick up. Usually something I said, or the *way* I said something, was the trigger. Unintentional disrespect, unknowingly stepping on the other guy's toes, is a common intrusion. When open interaction wanes and tension intervenes, I find the best way to approach the problem is head on. Confronting a minor problem before it escalates into a calamity helps insure success: "I feel a little tension in the air. Did I say something that offended you? Is there a problem?" I flush out the seeds of discontent before they germinate into full-grown, deep-rooted weeds! It never hurts to clear the air. Sometimes my perceptions are wrong and my concerns ill-founded. No matter. The reassurance that all is well helps me proceed.

THE AGONY OF VICTORY

For many, victory is the end point of a deal. Hostile, pressuring, and domineering, these people impose their will on others, especially when dealing from a strong power base. This is often the style of the wealthy individual or corporation. The power base provided by money is unquestionably one of the most misused. Suspicion verging on paranoia abounds: "Everyone is after my money." The reaction is often severe. The affluent tend to become closed, guarded, and insensitive. They distrust everyone, guarding their emotions to avoid becoming vulnerable to the jackals they constantly perceive snapping at their heels. When dealing with others, they attack and intimidate. To better insulate themselves, they totally strip others of their integrity, grinding them into submission. They couldn't care less about the needs of others — it is safest to leave them nothing! Continually having the upper hand in *all relationships* feeds their egos and preserves their power. The result is agony. Living in constant fear of others trying to usurp their power, they become angry and resentful. As their hostility mounts, they continually insulate themselves from their own emotions and the impact of others. This walling-off process leaves them distant and unresponsive. The result is a person impregnated with characteristics that are practically *guaranteed* to be unsuccessful in long-term interactions, jeopardizing the very power base he is striving so hard to protect. This activity is self-defeating. Money can be a useful tool for attaining objectives and can, indeed, provide a secure power base if properly utilized. It provides its owner with flexibility in timing decisions. He does not *have* to act, but can wait until conditions are favorable to his ends. But if he seeks victory, if he must vanquish to *feel* he has succeeded, then he has most assuredly lost!

2. Negotiating Tools

To be a successful negotiator, a particular attitude must be mastered. I have outlined the characteristics of a good negotiator, now let's have a look at how these can be put to use. These traits form a solid platform for implementing the techniques of negotiating. We will now discuss how these are put to work in mutual problem solving. A brief summary follows each section.

UNCONDITIONAL REGARD

Negotiation is a two-way street, and I must not discount the other person. His goals are just as real as my own and, by keeping them foremost in my mind, I have the greatest chance of harmoniously resolving our mutual desires. I maintain a high level of respect. This regard is *not conditional* on the personality traits or behavior of my negotiating partner.* I don't have to like

---

* I use the term "negotiating partner" to describe the other parties in a negotiation. The term "adversary" would typically be used, but thinking in that way fosters a negative attitude and is counterproductive.

someone to give him unconditional regard. It's a state of mind. So long as I don't judge him, don't moralize about the "rightness" or "wrongness" of his position, I can continue to preserve a positive, problem-solving air in the negotiation. I have found that as soon as I start judging, I am lost. My disapproval is quickly noticed, and the tone of the interplay sours. There is no right or wrong! Obviously, each person perceives his position as being correct. So both sides are "right," even if their ambitions are mutually exclusive. Moralizing just gets in the way of problem solving. Thinking in terms of right and wrong leads to win-lose games. It's nonproductive.

Summary: 1) Maintain a high regard for your negotiating partner, regardless of his personality or behavior.
2) Avoid judging. He needn't share your moral code.
3) Remember that your partner's goals are just as real as yours: There is no right or wrong.

NONVERBAL EXPRESSION

A major portion of any communication is nonverbal. What is transmitted by eye, hand, body, and tone of voice will greatly influence the negotiating environment and eventual outcome. I like to sit with my hands at my sides or on the table in front of me. I avoid crossing my arms over my chest, a defensive, standoffish posture. I maintain eye contact. This not only keeps me in close personal contact with my partner, but also better enables me to perceive subtle mood changes. I am not afraid to touch my partner when appropriate, as when giving recognition or reassurance. My voice is level and soft; reassuring, yet confident. My body is usually re- laxed, and leaning slightly toward my partner. The ob- jective is to facilitate openness, warmth, and respect.

Summary: 1) Nonverbal expression can greatly facilitate the negotiating climate.
2) An open, relaxed demeanor is best.
3) Maintain eye contact as much as possible.
4) Touch your partner when appro- priate.
5) Use a soft, level, confident tone of voice.

ACTIVE LISTENING

Before any problem can be resolved successfully, I must first understand the nature of the problem. Many negotiations break down before they get off the ground because one side or the other has not accurately per- ceived a position. Until I really know what the other guy wants, I can't begin to fill his needs. To help sort things out, I listen. I listen to the words and tone of voice. I observe the position of the body and the facial expressions. I try to take in the *whole* message being transmitted, not just the words. When the message has been delivered, I clarify what I have heard by repeating it.

Emotions are usually communicated nonverbally, yet they are equally as important as the verbal message, if not more so. In a recent real-estate project, the builder was late in finishing some of the improvements he had promised. We had a meeting.

"You got a damn good deal," he said. His tone was attacking, his body tense.

"You're feeling angry because you think you sold the building too cheaply, is that it?" I asked gently.

"Yeah, that's right! You stole the building, and now you want me to spend more time on it. I'm busy. I've got other projects to work on where I can *really* make some money," he said in clipped tones.

Again, I clarified: "You're feeling resentful about the deal we made, so you've decided not to do some work you previously agreed to. Is that what you're saying?"

"I stick to my agreements," he blurted.

"I understand your frustration," I continued. "Property values have skyrocketed since our deal and I can see why you'd be very eager to work on other projects. I know you are a man of your word. When can you comfortably finish the work?"

"Well, if you could give me thirty days, it would really help," he said, now noticeably more relaxed.

"That's fine," I said. "Thirty days will give you enough time to get a leg up on work in progress and finish my job at the same time?"

"Yeah," he said easily, now smiling. "That'll take the pressure off."

"Good! I'll instruct the escrow company that we

intend to close in thirty days," I said. "That way they can have all the papers drawn up and release the balance of the funds they are holding. I'll really be happy when this deal is put to bed. Then we can both concentrate our energy on other things."

By using active listening I was able to resolve both our needs without making waves. This could have turned into a messy situation. If I had become defensive, threatening to confiscate the funds in escrow through legal channels, or if I had counterattacked, questioning the builder's integrity, I not only would have delayed accomplishing my goal of completion of the project, but would also have seriously jeopardized our future relationship. As soon as the builder realized that I grasped *his* problem, and understood his frustration, he immediately relaxed. He had been prepared for a fight; his body posture and tone of voice telegraphed his anger and frustration. As a result of my understanding his plight and giving him accurate feedback, he quickly backed off and came up with a graceful out. He did not want to alienate me, but felt trapped. By not judging him and by not reacting to his emotional onslaught, I was able to facilitate an amicable resolution to the immediate problem and preserve the relationship.

Don't be afraid of affect. As soon as a discussion heats up and emotions start to boil, most people retreat, unable to deal with the situation. There is no need for fear. Tune in to what your partner is communicating and clarify his feelings, using active listening techniques. Feelings change. He won't stay angry forever. Your posture in a negotiation will be markedly strengthened if you learn to stay with people during emotional on-slaught. You will gain their respect and confidence and accomplish your goals.

On the other hand, learn to control your own anger. It severely weakens your negotiating position. Saladin, a famed sultan of Islam during the Crusades, once led his forces into battle. Shortly after the battle began, this renowned fighter and fearless leader returned to his tent. When asked by his aides what was wrong, he said, "I feel angry. I never fight when I feel angry. It makes me blind and weak." The same is true of negotiations. To be effective you need to have all your wits about you, to feel centered. Anger masks reason. When you feel it, postpone your discussions and return to your tent.

Summary: 1) Listen to the *whole* message being communicated by your negotiating partner. His tone of voice, body talk, and expressions are as important as his words.

2) Feed back to him what you have heard by summarizing the message.

3) Avoid reacting to an emotional attack.

4) When your negotiating partner comes up with a meaningful resolution to a problem, give him immediate positive reinforcement (see following heading).

5) Don't be afraid of affect.
6) Learn to control your own emotions, especially anger.

POSITIVE FEEDBACK

In the preceeding example the builder, after having what he was communicating fed back to him and not liking what he was hearing, retreated to a more constructive posture. Remember, it was *he* who suggested the thirty-day deadline for completion. That was the kind of positive action I was looking for. The fact that he made the suggestion greatly increased the chances of his meeting the deadline. If I had made the suggestion and he had demurred, my position would have been much weaker, the probability of results diminished. When he made the suggestion, he took responsibility for his actions. If I had set the terms and he failed to meet the deadline, it would have been *my* idea that failed, not his. He could say that he had tried, but that I had just not given him enough time. When I allowed him to come up with a solution and set a deadline, he accepted responsibility and the likelihood of success skyrocketed.

I did take an active role, however, in reinforcing his idea. I accomplished this in two ways. First, I agreed this was a good solution. He need go no farther, he had my support. I took the next step, giving instructions to the escrow company to draw up the closing papers in accordance with his plan. Now an independent third party was involved, increasing the builder's responsibilities. In addition, I brought up the pleasant subject of his receiving the balance of his compensation (tangible reward) and speculated on how good we would both feel when the project was complete (intangible reward).

Summary: 1) Whenever possible, let your negotiating partner come up with possible solutions to problems.

2) When a solution is acceptable, give him immediate positive reinforcement of *his* idea.

3) Set up a chain of events (preferably involving outside parties) dependent on implementation of his solution.

4) Give him immediate reward ("That's a good idea") and, when relevant, point out the future rewards of successfully carrying out his plan.

SETTING OBJECTIVES

An important part of most negotiations is determining *when* agreements will be fulfilled. Many deals drag on endlessly because time objectives have not been clearly determined. Some deals fall through altogether. Once a basic agreement is made, I make sure all parties understand their temporal obligations. I find it best to let my negotiating partners set their own objectives. The strategy here parallels that of allowing them to come up with ideas that I positively reinforce. In this case we continue to chew on schedules until *they* come up with one that best suits our mutual needs.

I encourage them to set *specific* target dates for the various phases of a project. We then set up dates to review their progress. This way a complex project is broken down into clear-cut, easily digestible small steps with periodic reviews of progress. I reinforce their objectives and record their conclusions in writing whenever possible. I don't like to push people. My best results come from allowing them to set their own pace, then periodically reviewing their progress.

Summary: 1) Set time objectives for completion of terms of an agreement.
2) Allow your negotiating partner to set his own schedule.
3) Reinforce the agreed-upon schedule both verbally and in writing.
4) Periodically review attainment of time parameters.

"I" LANGUAGE

One of the most effective techniques in any form of human communication is the use of "I" language. Put simply, it is the use of the word "I" rather than "you." This helps to avoid making judgments and accusations, while more accurately communicating feeling. There is a big difference between the two sentences: "You make me feel uncomfortable" and "I feel uncomfortable." The former is an accusation; the latter a statement of feeling without blame. An accusation is likely to stir up a strong negative reaction; the statement of feeling instills empathy and concern. A common tangible example occurs when your negotiating partner has a different understanding of an agreement than you do. One approach would be: "You're wrong! That's not what we agreed to." This judgment is likely to evoke a defensive or competitive response. Far more effective would be a statement such as: "*I*'m confused. That's not *my* understanding. Didn't we agree that . . ." This approach is likely to lead to a speedy, cooperative resolution.

Dealing with emotions is a significant part of any negotiation. As we have seen, active listening will help your negotiating partner sort out *his* emotions. "I" language will help you communicate *your* feelings. When I tell my partner I'm frustrated, afraid, sad, resentful, relieved, excited, happy, or satisfied, I find it strengthens our relationship, makes it more real, more human. It elevates it beyond just a business dealing, personalizing it. But remember to start each sentence with an "I." "I'm afraid" is very different from "You scare me."

Don't confuse "I feel" with "I think." "I feel that you are wrong" is *not* a statement of feeling!

Summary: 1) Make "I" statements, not "you" statements.

2) Don't hesitate to communicate true feelings as long as you start with "I feel."

3) Don't say "I feel" when you really mean "I think."

40

INGRATIATE YOURSELF

The importance of maintaining a positive atmosphere has been stressed. My experience has been that the initial meeting with my negotiating partner is the most crucial for setting the stage for our interaction. Warmth and cordiality expressed early set the tempo for a cooperative spirit. A topic of conversation that makes *my partner* comfortable is a good starting point. My endeavors are directed toward relaxing *him*, making conversation easy. When appropriate, I give him positive support and recognition. I want him to feel important; I want to elevate his self-esteem; I want him to feel good when he is dealing with me so that he eagerly looks forward to our meetings rather than dreading them.

At subsequent meetings I always attempt to begin the discussions with topics that provide him with solid footing. Rewarding him for work accomplished, or objectives met on time, is a fruitful opening. Listening to and understanding *his* problems, and letting him know I have understood them (active listening) provides subsequent reinforcement. Once a cooperative problem-solving mode has been established, it is much easier for me to ease the discussion around to my concerns (using "I" language), and my chances for successful resolution are enhanced. Compliments and recognition are excellent tools. Remember, the better your partner feels about himself, the better he will feel about you.

Small gifts or favors go a long way toward cementing relationships. I have found that the more I can do for someone in little personal services, the easier it is for me to accomplish major objectives (remember the water doggies).

Summary: 1) Initial meetings are paramount for setting the tone of negotiations.
2) Do everything in your power to ingratiate yourself with your negotiating partner at an early stage.
3) Start each meeting with a subject that provides a solid footing for your partner.
4) Freely use compliments, recognition, reward, and thoughtful personal services.

ADAPTING TO DIFFERENT PERSONALITY TYPES

The techniques outlined thus far will help you deal with a wide range of personalities. Active listening and "I" language are applicable to every negotiation, and will help you stay centered. I do vary my demeanor, however, depending upon the behavior of my partner. With the typically aggressive "business type" I focus on calming and soothing, lowering my voice and speaking slowly and directly. With introverted types I spend more time on neutral issues, allowing them to come out of their shells slowly as their confidence increases. With passive types I try to kindle their enthusiasm, increasing their involvement. "Wheeler-dealers" must be slowed down and made to clarify their positions. I try to turn hot air into concrete, often a difficult metamorphosis. With skillful negotiators, proficient in these techniques, I quickly cut through the preliminaries and get down to problem solving. I have learned to recognize talent early and find that, once mutual respect has been established, we can get right to the meat of the issues. Such negotiations are usually brief and to the point, both sides knowing when to yield.

Summary: 1) Adapt your style to your partner, neutralizing aggressiveness and stimulating passivity.
2) When dealing with a talented negotiator, get down to details as soon as mutual respect has been established.

HOW TO DEAL WITH ANIMOSITY

It is a natural reaction for human beings to be contrary. For confirmation, monitor a discussion with your spouse or child. Odds are, whatever you say, they will voice the opposite opinion.

It is a psychological fact that even friendly people generally look for an opposing viewpoint. When animosity exists, this tendency is exacerbated. Then *whatever* you say is wrong. This knowledge can be useful when negotiating with a hostile party. You can't win. Everything you say will be challenged. Knowing this, argue the converse of your desired goals. Since whatever you say must be wrong, your negotiating partner will unwittingly begin to argue the position you desire. Hang in tough for a while, then let him have *his* way.

Summary: 1) People have a natural tendency to be contrary.
2) Animosity increases this inclination.
3) Arguing the opposing case in these situations can produce the results you desire.

COMPROMISE: WHEN AND HOW TO YIELD

Sometimes negotiations reach an impasse, a point at which the parties' needs are mutually exclusive. Working through this impasse is often most difficult. Flexibility is required on both sides. Unresolved issues are usually multifaceted. They are not simple problems, but can be broken down into component parts. Naturally, some concessions will be less painful than others. It is important to sort out priorities clearly in your mind, and to ferret out accurately the order of importance to your partner. An issue that is of minor consequence to you may be a major concession in his mind. If so, don't give it up lightly! If he views it as a major concession, make sure he knows that you are aware it is a major concession, and ask for *quid pro quo*. I have seen negotiators get themselves into untenable positions by yielding too easily on matters of relative unimportance to them, severely compromising their bargaining position. By having both your priorities and those of your partner clearly in mind, it's much easier to shuffle things around and make the cards come together into a neat deck.

Summary: 1) When a negotiation reaches an impasse, make sure you clearly understand both your partner's priorities and your own.

2) When you make a major concession (in your partner's eyes), make sure he is aware that you know it is a major concession and get appropriate compensation.

AVOID PRECONCEPTIONS

I find it helpful to avoid preconceived notions of what my negotiating partner is likely to come up with. Such prejudices may unnecessarily color my response, compromising the tone of the parlay. Far better to just sit back and listen without reacting. If he comes up with a totally unsatisfactory solution, I do not jump down his throat. Rather, I listen and clarify, making absolutely sure I have understood his offer. If he proposes a solution far better than my expectations, I react the same way, clarifying, listening, and understanding. Only after I have absorbed all his output, and digested it, will I respond. This often will be at a subsequent meeting. I avoid being precipitous. Blurting out an emotional response has ruined many a deal! It's like having pitched eight perfect innings, then throwing a home-run pitch that not only spoils the no-hitter, but blows the game as well.

Summary: 1) Avoid preconceived notions of what your negotiating partner will suggest.

2) Don't react, either positively or negatively, to concrete proposals. Clarify, listen, and understand.

3) Thoroughly digest ideas before responding.

REACTING VERSUS INITIATING

It is usually preferable, as we have seen, to let your negotiating partner come up with all the answers. Allowing him to take the initiative increases his sense of participation, responsibility, and commitment. The more ideas that are his, the better. Your role should be to provide support and to channel and fine-tune his energies. This does not mean that you simply sit, vacantly staring out the window. Your role is critical. When he veers off course, you must bring him back on target; when he bogs down, you must get him going again. To do this, in addition to the techniques already mentioned, you should use open-ended questioning: "You mentioned that there might be ways to cut costs by economies of scale. I'd like to pursue that a little more." Or, "If we do it the way you suggest, what drawbacks do you see?" The skillful negotiator helps his partner focus his thoughts by keeping him chewing on his constructs until he spontaneously realizes their weaknesses. It is much less effective to point out drawbacks. This may lead him to a defensive position. By asking a series of general questions, I allow my partner to think his arguments through, following them to their logical conclusions. Often he will come up spontaneously with flaws in his thinking, revising his position into a much more palatable format.

Not long ago a man approached me with an attractive real-estate package. The deal involved converting existing apartments to condominiums. It required $250,000 of investment capital. The guy who had put it together had everything arranged — except the capital.

We started to negotiate. The project looked as if it would yield about $150,000 in eighteen months, assuming no flies in the ointment. I personally did not want to invest such sums in a single project, but had clients who could easily swallow it.

I asked, "How do you want to structure things?"

He said, "You raise the money. We will both be general partners, the investors limited partners. The general partners will take half the deal; the limited partners half. I will take two-thirds of the general-partner interest for putting the deal together and seeing it through and give you one-third for raising the money. Okay?"

"I don't know," I said. "What are the risks?"

"There are no risks," he said forcefully. "It's a sure thing!"

I responded, "Then, if I understand you correctly, you're saying that there is no way the investors can lose their money and that the hundred and fifty thousand profit is a certainty. Is that right?"

"Well, just about. I've got the zoning already. The area is booming."

"What could *possibly* go wrong?" I asked.

"Well, it *could* cost more to convert it than we have budgeted. We *may* not be able to sell the condominiums for as much as we anticipate. The real-estate market *could* soften, making marketing difficult and drawn out. But none of this is likely."

"You say you already have the zoning?" I asked.

"Not in my hands. But I've done these before and I have close friends at City Hall," he answered.

"In other words, the zoning change is probable but not definite. Is that right?"

"Say, ninety percent probable," he said.

"And if the ten percent wins out?"

"If I don't get the zoning, the deal loses a lot of its attractiveness. We'd be lucky to break even," he answered more pensively.

"Is there any way to reduce the risk?'" I asked.

He thought for a while, then said, "I suppose we could make the zoning change a condition of escrow. The current owner could file for the change, and we could bear the expenses. Would only cost a few thousand."

"That's a good idea," I said, encouraging him. "Now, about the split . . ."

"You think two-thirds one-third is too rich, huh?" (I hesitated, not responding.) "Okay, fifty-fifty," he said.

"I'm concerned about the investors' exposure," I asserted, changing the subject. "How do you intend to structure the general partners' fifty-percent interest in the project?"

"They get fifty percent of the deal and we get fifty percent," he retorted.

"And if there are no profits?"

"I see your point," he said. (I was unaware that I had made a point.) "Yeah, we'll have to structure it so that we get fifty percent of the *profits*, not fifty percent of the deal. Otherwise, if it flopped, we'd be entitled to fifty percent of the investors' initial investment. That's not right."

"So where are we now?" I asked.

"Well, you raise the money. We'll lower the risk by making the zoning change a condition of escrow. The partnership will be set up so that the general partners get fifty percent of the profits, not a fifty-percent-ownership interest. And you and I will be equal partners—fifty-fifty."

"Fine. I agree. How shall we finalize our understanding?" I asked.

"I'll have my attorney draw up an agreement," he said.

"All right. When shall we meet to sign it?"

"A week will be plenty of time," he said.

"I'll meet you here one week from today," I said, smiling. We shook hands and the meeting was over.

An analysis of the dynamics of this negotiation shows that all I did was ask questions. *All* the ideas originated from my partner. I facilitated his thought process, but *he* came up with all the solutions. When he had it all together, I agreed to *his* conditions.

Summary: 1) Reacting is much more effective than initiating.

2) Reacting does not mean being passive. Take an active role in directing your partner's energies toward problem solving.

3) Use general questions to steer the discussions in a productive direction.

4) Avoid giving opinions.

5) Support sound conclusions by your partner.

THE ASSUMPTIVE POSTURE

As with most rules, there are exceptions to the reactive posture. Occasionally, it is more effective to be assumptive. A business associate of mine told me about an extraordinarily low rate he had received on an income-property mortgage from a savings and loan. I had had several dealings with this association, but was not even in the same league as my associate. I invited my loan officer to lunch. During the course of our meal I mentioned a piece of property I wanted financed. Amiably, he told me he would provide the money.

"What are your *standard* rates on this type project?" I asked.

"Nine and three-quarters to ten percent," he answered without hesitation.

I knew that my associate had received a 9¼-percent rate on a similar project. I took the assumptive approach: "So your *preferred* clients, then, would get a nine and one-quarter rate?"

Momentarily taken aback, he nodded.

"That sounds a lot better," I said. "It makes the deal do-able."

"Of course, if you sell the project, the rate will become nine and three-quarters," he said, recovering quickly. "The new client will not be preferred."

"Understood and agreed."

It would have been exceedingly difficult for the loan officer to have told me I was not a preferred client (although I had never claimed to be one; I just assumed it). I clearly knew the rates bestowed upon the favored. By taking the assumptive posture, I caught the loan officer a little off guard and achieved my objective. I have been a preferred client ever since.

Summary: 1) Occasionally it is useful to take an assumptive posture.

2) This is often true when you have information that your negotiating partner does not know you have.

3) Be smooth and graceful when making assumptions.

4) Be ready to close the deal promptly if your assumption is accepted.

KEEPING NEEDS CLEAR

Since negotiation is a dynamic process, I continually evaluate my needs and the needs of my partner.

These may change during the course of the interaction. *Objectively* evaluating and re-evaluating my own needs, and the needs of others, is necessary for me to know where I am and where I want to go. As talks proceed, it is easy to get caught up in specifics and lose sight of broad objectives. I find that standing back a moment and looking at the process help me get a clearer picture of what's really going on. These momentary pauses allow me to redirect my thinking, if necessary, and bring the discussions back on line if they have deviated.

Summary: 1) Objectively evaluate and periodically reassess your needs and the needs of your partner.
2) Step back, from time to time, and examine your progress, evaluating the dynamics of your interaction and determining whether the process is on course.
3) Make appropriate adjustments if you have deviated, or if needs have changed.

THE USE OF "PARTNERS"

When finalizing a deal, I often want a little time to review the situation. Experience tells me that, when I go home and review matters, I sometimes have second thoughts. If I come back the next day voicing newfound reservations, my negotiating partner may fly off the handle. From his point of view we had the makings of a deal; now I'm changing terms and conditions. His reaction may be severe, and the negotiations compromised. A good agreement can be blown at this stage. To avoid all these nasties, I leave myself an out. Instead of saying, "Let me go home and sleep on this," I say, "This sounds good to me, but I have to review it with *my partners.*" In almost every situation it is plausible to have silent partners. My posture becomes that of an intermediary. If I return to the negotiating table with reservations, they are not mine but my partners'. I can calmly and objectively explain my partners' position with relatively little risk. It is inappropriate for the person with whom I'm negotiating to blow up, because another variable, removed from either of us, is the source of new input. I am in position to mediate between my negotiating partner and my "partners." In effect, I am the mediator between the initial position and the new position. The result is usually a satisfactory compromise.

Summary: 1) When considering an agreement, limit your authority by saying you must review it with your "partners."

2) If you have second thoughts about some provisions, point these out as reservations of your associates.

3) Proceed to negotiate between the old position and the preferred position, acting as a mediator.

CORPORATE NEEDS VS. INDIVIDUAL NEEDS

When dealing with someone who represents a corporation, it is prudent to distinguish between his personal needs and the needs of his corporation. If I can fill his personal needs, especially his intangible ones, he may see his way clear to work with me on how best to present our position to his superiors in the light of corporate objectives. An excellent example of this is the discussions I had with my broker when commissions on stock transactions became negotiable (see chapter on Stocks, p. 58). My broker's need was to get cash in his pocket; his company's need was to give the broker as little as possible, and to charge the client as much as he would stomach. The less the firm pays its salesmen, the more room it has to negotiate with clients. My needs were to pay as little as possible. Theoretically, it didn't matter how my payment was divided up.

This negotiation had two prongs. The first, filling the needs of the broker. Obviously, to meet my objectives he would have to settle for a smaller percentage than he was used to. But within the general framework of taking less, I wanted him to get as much as possible. *Together* we devised a plan to approach his corporate superiors. His approach was to present my actual operating history over the years. This was a juicy, trouble-free account that required practically no research support. He pointed out that the firm had little to do but execute orders. He suggested he should have a slightly larger slice of the pie because I was a "retail" client, even though I did more volume than many institutions. When the smoke cleared, they reached a compromise:

the corporation taking less than normal, the broker less than he had asked, but more than he had originally expected. Naturally, he attributed part of his success to me, and has since liberally returned the favor with "hot" new issues and the like.

I probably could have squeezed out a little more if I had really pushed. The broker might have taken still less. I think this would have been a serious error in judgment. First, he would have been far less motivated to negotiate with his bosses. He might have taken a hard line. Negotiations could have bogged down early. Second, even if I had been "successful" in getting my way, he would most likely have felt some resentment that might have come out in subtle ways, like overlooking my name when there was easy money to be made or an "inside" tip to be whispered. By not demanding the whole loaf, I was able to eat more bread.

Summary: 1) When dealing with someone who represents a corporation, distinguish between his personal needs and the needs of his company.
2) Fill his personal needs, then work together to figure out how to present your case to his superiors.

THE RISK TECHNIQUE

The risk technique, as the name implies, is not the world's safest technique. Therefore it should be used judiciously. The technique involves pointing out all the reasons why a negotiation should be abandoned, exaggerating how *bad* everything is, and pointing out why it is impossible to continue. By being even more negative than your partner is at his worst, you often convert him into a position of defending the *benefits* of the negotiation instead of the drawbacks: "Things aren't as bad as all that. There's a lot to be said for continuing our dealings . . ." Often this will break an impasse and lead to a constructive solution. The risk is that your partner will say, "You're right. Let's stop. This is getting us nowhere."

When employing the risk technique, you must be prepared for this potentiality. For this reason, I usually use it only as a last resort. The exception is when you are dealing with an extremely aggressive, argumentative person who really has no intention of withdrawing from a deal, but whose style is to attack. In this instance, your partner is caught totally unawares and he will quickly start backpedaling so as not to blow the deal. This technique has turned many a lion into a pussycat.

Summary: 1) The risk technique is a sudden reversal of posture, dramatically pointing out why a negotiation should be abandoned.

2) When using this technique you must be prepared for the consequences. It may mark the end of a negotiation.

3) This technique is especially effec-

tive with people who come on strong but who, in reality, could not possibly be persuaded to abandon a deal.

II

The Stock Market

A WINNING FORMULA*

● Readers of this book probably own or have owned securities at some time or another. Odds are they have lost money at this game — most so-called small investors have taken a bath in the stock market. The 1973–1974 stock market debacle sent the little guy scurrying for the sidelines where he still remains, comfortably out of bounds so he can't be hurt. Like a prairie dog in his burrow he will huddle, motionless, until he feels the financial threat has passed, then, tenuously, once again begin to nibble at securities. By this time the upturn in the economic cycle will have finally salved the wounds of 1969–1974. Overwhelmed by a hunger for money and piquant stories of stock-market coups from acquaintances, he will once again throw himself into the breach — and once again get zapped!

If this description matches your history, you shouldn't feel *too* bad. You've got some pretty impressive company: all those master-minds that shepherd the

*A glossary of terms used in this chapter is provided on page 225.

billions of dollars invested in mutual fund and pension trusts are also usually wrong. So are the banks and insurance companies. If all these giants are also traversing a slippery slope, who, then, reaps the profits? The best performance award goes to the members of the New York Stock Exchange for managing their own portfolios. Within this elite group the pole position goes to the specialist.

For those unfamiliar, a specialist is an individual who sits on the floor of the stock exchange, and whose function (theoretically) is to "provide an orderly market in the purchase and sale of securities." Each listed stock on, say, the New York Stock Exchange is represented by a specialist. All buy and sell orders for the stocks he supervises pass through his books. He is permitted to acquire shares for his own account or sell shares short, all in the interest of maintaining an orderly market. Sounds pretty reasonable so far, right? Except for one thing — greed! Do you really believe that these wizened, gnarled veterans are going to perform their orderly duties without regard for personal gain? Altruistic these gnomes are not! And they are as clever as a diamond merchant evaluating a perfect stone for a recently widowed woman who hasn't a clue as to its value. When Chase Manhattan is accumulating stock, they must do it through our friendly specialist. When "The Rock" wants to sell a piece, Prudential's order eventually crosses the specialist's book.

So *how* does the specialist maintain an orderly market? If he is long stock (and he usually is if the stock is going up) he gradually liquidates his position to keep the price of the stock from rising *too* fast. If he is short stock, he covers his position as the stock is declining to keep the downward trend from being *too* precipitous. Of course, he profits handsomely from these transactions — but all for the cause of an orderly market.

If these financial wizards are usually right, and they are, then how could I share their privileged knowledge? I quickly discarded the idea of their confiding in me voluntarily. I began to research the subject and found a number of technical analysts also had a great deal of interest in the activity of the specialists and New York Stock Exchange members, but that the significance of these reports was diluted in a morass of graphs, charts, trend lines, advance-decline lines, momentum studies, and the like.

I decided to discard these and home in on the activities of the specialists and members. I went through a mass of data covering a twenty-five-year span. The distillate I culled is this: stock market movement is highly predictable and is inversely proportional to specialist and New York Stock Exchange members short sales. Put more simply — *if the specialists and members are selling short, the market tends to go down; when their shorting dries up, probabilities favor a market rally.**

A short sale is the sale of stock without prior ownership. In other words, to sell short you reverse the normal process. Instead of buying first and later selling,

---

* I want to stress that this is not an original concept. This correlation was first discovered by a Berkeley, California, group some years ago.

you sell first and buy back later. To gauge specialist and member shorting you must relate their short sales to total short sales, since the figures only have significance *relative* to how much shorting is being done by others presumably less sophisticated. The figures for who is doing what in the way of shorting are published weekly on the inside back page of Monday's *Wall Street Journal* under the heading, "Odd-Lot Trading." (See Illustration A.) The key column in this illustration is the one headed "short sales." Total short sales include everybody — all institutions, the specialists, you, me, etc. Then specialist and member short sales are broken out separately. In this illustration total short sales were 6,117,620 shares. Of these, the specialists accounted for 2,589,100 shares

ILLUSTRATION A

November 15, 1976—*Wall Street Journal*

	Purchases	Sales (incl. Short Sales)	*Short Sales**
Total	79,165,180	79,165,180	*6,117,620*
For Member Accounts:**			
As Specialists:	9,368,640	10,682,490	*2,589,100*
As Floor Traders:	387,400	496,180	*106,700*
Others (except as Odd-lot Dealers)	8,901,322	8,462,218	*2,077,190*

* Italics are the author's.

** The sum of Specialists, Floor Traders, and Others equals the New York Stock Exchange member activities.

or 42 percent. The members include the specialists, floor traders, and "others." These are tabulated under the heading "for Member Accounts." In this example the members accounted for 4,772,990 shares, or 78 percent. Naturally, a one-week figure may be spurious, so I use a four-week moving average (add the current week's figures to the previous three weeks and divide by four).

WHEN TO BUY

The magic buy numbers are 40 percent and 65 percent. When the specialist is short 40 percent or less of the total short sales and the members are short 65 percent or less — *BUY!!* The market is about to take off! History bears this out. These experts would have put the Delphic oracle to shame with the accuracy of their prophecies. Since 1970 the running average has reached this target on two occasions: May, 1970 and September, 1974.

In May, 1970, the Dow Jones Industrial Average (DJIA) stood at about 700. In the next twelve months it zoomed up an incredible two hundred and forty points to 940! The next time the indicators hit the magic numbers was September, 1974. The Dow was just over 600. Again the popular index soared two hundred points in a year! Astounding!

The specialists and the members almost always think alike. In May, 1970, and September, 1974, the short sales for both groups were very low relative to other investors. In October, 1976, however, they diverged dramatically: the specialists were short 38 percent, the members 78 percent. The specialist figure was a raging buy sign, while the member figure indicated caution. This dissonance was difficult to fathom and my history over the previous ten years provided no precedent for handling this dichotomy. I decided to buy stocks cautiously, closely monitoring the weekly figures for both groups. The market rallied sharply, tacking on one hundred points in two months. During this time both the specialists and members became more bearish, despite the financial community's chorus of new highs. When the Dow hit new all-time highs (at the 1020 level), the papers and newscasts were filled with predictions of 1150 or more. The members, however, had become clearly negative on the market. They were short 82 percent of the stock. Above 80 percent is a sell signal. The specialists were short 42 percent of the stock, slightly on the bullish side.

Still confused and having fat profits, I sold 80 percent of my holdings. At the time of this writing, December, 1977, the members are *still* bearish. They continue to short 80 percent or more of the weekly total. The specialists, on the other hand, have been short less than 45 percent throughout 1977. The industrial averages are at 815. It appears that the specialists were correct for the two-month period ending December, 1976, and the members have been right since. Even though I was lucky and made money during this period, this experience has taught me to wait before buying until *both* the specialists and the members flash a buy signal. Even though the averages have dropped over 200 points from

December, 1976, to December, 1977, I still think we have farther to go on the downside. The members continue to short 84 percent despite the drop.

WHEN TO SELL

I sell when specialist short sales are 60 percent of the total short sales and member sales are 80 percent of the total on a running four-week average. The stocks I bought in May and June, 1970, were sold in April, 1971 (magic numbers 61 percent and 82 percent). The stocks I bought in September and October, 1974, I sold in February, 1976 (60 percent and 80 percent). I was out of the market from April, 1971, to September, 1974, and from February, 1976, until November, 1976.* (Illustration B summarizes buy-sell points and respective DJIA figures.)

SELLING SHORT

Americans are fundamentally optimistic. We are used to prosperity and growth and expect them to continue indefinitely. Sure, there may be a short pause here and there, but we like to believe the trend is always up. Not so! Our economy is cyclical — a growth spurt leads to escalating prices, scarce supplies of raw materials, and inflation. This is remedied by tightening the reins on the money supply by increasing interest rates, which results in a slowdown in business activity, and waning

---

* By "out of the market" I mean not long stock. During part of this time I invested in bonds, and wrote covered stock options (see headings entitled, "When to Write Covered Options," and, "When to Buy Bonds").

ILLUSTRATION B

Date	Dow Jones Industrial Average	Specialist Short Sales Ratio	New York Stock Exchange Member Short Sale Ratio	Buy/Sell Signal
May 1970	710	40%	60%	BUY
April 1971	920	61%	82%	SELL
September 1974	600	39%	61%	BUY
February 1976	980	60%	80%	SELL
October 1976	960	38%*	78%*	BUY/ CAUTION
December 1976	1022	42%*	82%*	HOLD/ SELL
December 1977	815	45%*	84%*	HOLD/ SELL

* Members have been bearish for the 14-month period ending December, 1977, while specialists have been bullish. After a sharp two-month surge, ending December, 1976, the market has steadily declined over 200 points, bearing out the steady NYSE member sell signals. In this unusual dichotomy between the specialists and the NYSE members, the members have won out.

consumer confidence. As demand slows, prices recede, and inventories are liquidated. The Federal Reserve Board then gradually opens the money spigot, interest rates fall, the money supply increases, the consumer begins to spend again, and the cycle repeats itself. True, these economic cycles are biased toward the positive side and the *very* long-range trend of our economy appears to be up.

Despite many ups and downs, most of our thinking is stuck on up. And our bank accounts are stuck on empty. This pattern of eternal optimism is patriotic, but it misses money-making opportunities. It is exceptionally difficult for most people to bet against everything being rosy. To even *think* that the stock market might go down, let alone risk money on it, makes you a Benedict Arnold in the eyes of many. But, perish the thought, it is sometimes correct (not to mention wise) to buck the trend and *go short* in the stock market — especially if you want to make money. Before you suggest that I relinquish my American citizenship let me allay your fears—selling short does not happen that often. Only once in the past ten years—way back in June, 1968 — have the signals warranted shorting. *When the specialist is short 65 percent or more and the members are short at least 85 percent of the total short sales it is time for you to short.* In 1968 the figures were 67 percent and 87 percent respectively.

Yes, I shorted stocks then (DJIA 900), and really needed the courage of my convictions to hang in there. As if to punish me for my negative thinking, the market took off on the upside, zooming eighty points in four and a half months. During this period I rechecked my calculations several times, pulled in my belt another couple of notches, and tried to travel to places that didn't get the *International Herald Tribune*. Each time I inadvertently caught up with a paper, a new horror awaited me. The worst was over by Thanksgiving, 1968, and by Christmas the market was in retreat. The year 1969 was a fine year to be short — the market plunged one hundred and fifty points. When the short indicator hit 45 percent in mid-April, 1970, I covered my shorts. The Dow stood at 750. It fell another fifty points or so after I covered, but I was quite pleased with my gains.

To summarize, I short stocks when the indicators hit 65 percent and 85 percent respectively on a four-week moving average. I cover my shorts when they hit 45 percent and 75 percent and I buy when they hit 40 percent and 65 percent, selling when they hit 60 percent and 80 percent. (Graph illustration C and D.)

For the past eight years I have been guided by this concept, averaging gains of 25 percent per year on my stock investments (*including* time out of the market). Mind you, the market as measured by the Dow Jones Industrial Averages has done *nothing* during this time span. The Dow hit 1000 in 1968 and is hovering in the low 800's at the time of this writing.

CHOOSING STOCKS

The worst of all possible worlds is to correctly predict the direction of the market, but choose stocks that underperform or, worse yet, move opposite to the general market. *The trick is to pick a stock that will*

ILLUSTRATION C

Specialist Short Sales as
Percentage of Total Short Sales

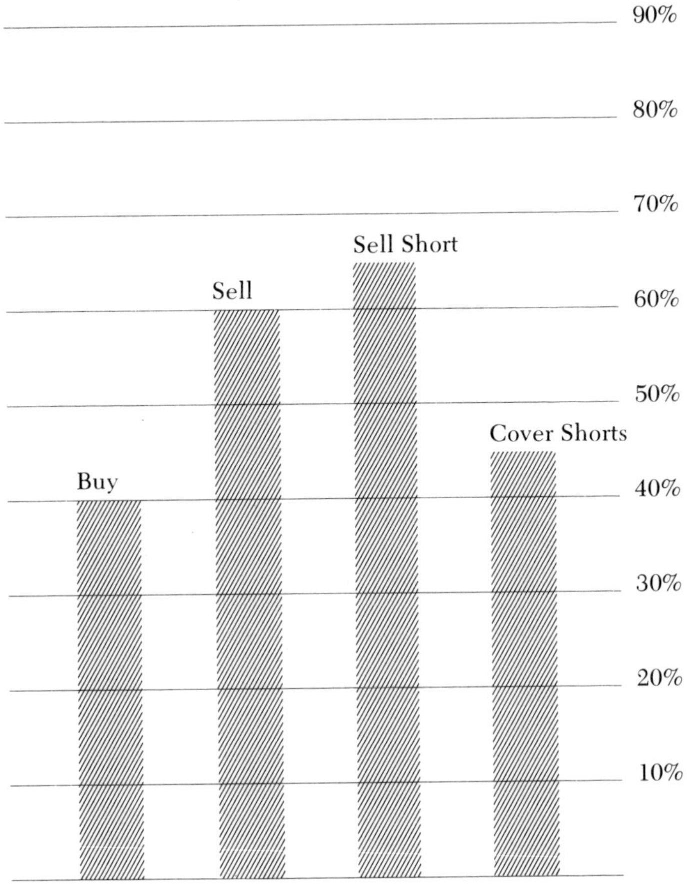

ILLUSTRATION D

NYSE Member Short Sales as
Percentage of Total Short Sales

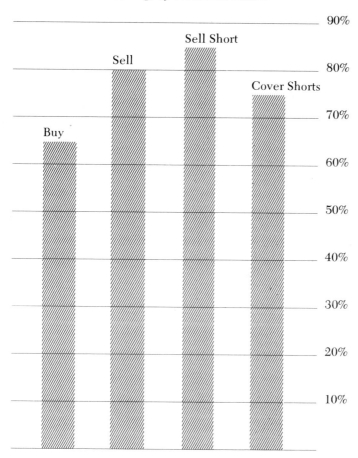

appreciate faster than the market when it's rising or a stock that declines faster than the market when the indicators dictate selling short.

Selecting individual stocks is more difficult than buy-sell timing decisions. But if a few basic rules are heeded, the task becomes measurably easier. Table I lists desirable stock characteristics and pitfalls to be avoided. During the time the market is trading in the neutral band of the "indicators," I watch stock performance. No, not all 1600 plus stocks on the New York Stock Exchange, but representative stocks (which I call "bellwether" stocks) from each industry group. Table II displays the industry with its bellwether stock. This does *not* necessarily mean that I buy, or sell short, the bellwether stock when it is time to act. Rather, I use these stocks only to isolate the *groups* most apt to respond according to the indicators. Next, I request of my brokers (I have several) detailed reports on individual companies within a designated group. These companies are then evaluated according to the parameters outlined in Table I:

TABLE I

Desired Characteristics	*Pitfalls*
1) No "clouds" over stock	Potentially serious unresolved problems
2) Steadily improving five-year growth in earnings	Erratic five-year earnings picture

Desired Characteristics	*Pitfalls*
3) Stock resists deterioration in sideways or down markets	Stock weak in sideways or down markets
4) Stock compatible with phase of market cycle	Stock growth incompatible with phase of business cycle
5) Stock likely to benefit from political & economic climate	Stock under pressure due to political decisions
6) Stock easily bought and sold	Small float — stock difficult to buy and sell
7) Active daily turnover	Sluggish daily turnover
8) Yield provides downside prop	Yield provides no downside protection

TABLE II

Industry	*Bellwether Stock(s)*
Aerospace	Boeing
Airlines	Delta
Aluminum	Alcoa
Appliances	Whirlpool
Banks	Citicorp
Brewers	Schlitz
Business Machines	IBM
Chemicals	Union Carbide
Coal	Pittston

TABLE II (*continued*)

Industry	*Bellwether Stock(s)*
Computer/Technology	Texas Instruments
Conglomerates	Teledyne
Copper	Phelps Dodge
Cosmetics	Revlon
Defense	Raytheon, General Dynamics
Drugs	Merck
Electronics & Broadcasting	RCA
Farm Equipment	Deere & Co.
Finance	MGIC
Forest Products	Weyerhaeuser
Gold	Dome
Hotel/Motel	Marriott
Insurance	Aetna Life & Casualty
Machinery	Caterpillar Tractor
Mobile Homes	Skyline
Motors	General Motors
Oil-Domestic	Atlantic Richfield
Oil-International	Exxon
Oil Service	Halliburton
Paper	International Paper
REIT'S	Equitable Life Mortgage
Restaurants	McDonald's
Retail	Sears, Kresge
Savings & Loans	Imperial Corp. of America, First Charter Financial

TABLE II (*continued*)

Industry	*Bellwether Stock(s)*
Soft Drinks	Coca-Cola
Steel	US Steel
Tires	Goodyear
Utilities	American Telephone

1) *Are there any clouds over the stocks?* Major lawsuits pending? Investigations by government regulatory bodies? Major problems in a key division? Management upheavals? Financing problems? Omitted or reduced dividends? In short, any major unresolved questions that could *drastically* affect stock performance.*

2) *Past performance.* Although past performance does not guarantee future growth, it sure helps point the way. Look at the five-year compound growth rate in earnings as compared with other stocks in the same industry. Momentum is a key word here; the stock market is an excellent example of Newtonian physics. Remember, "an object in motion tends to remain in motion; an object at rest tends to remain at rest." If a company has maintained a 15-percent compound growth rate over the past five years, odds favor continuation of this trend. Predictability is important. I much prefer orderly, steady, year-to-year increases to roller-coaster gains and quick reversals. A company that is up 30 percent one year and down 15 percent the next is much more likely to be labeled with skull and crossbones in my rating

* Lawsuits and other contingent liabilities are usually noted in the footnotes of the financial statements in a company's annual report.

system than one characterized by a 12–18 percent *steady* compound growth rate. Part of my strategy involves sleeping nights!

3) *Performance during a market correction.* Periodic downward bursts occur when the primary trend of the market is up. The converse is also true. It is useful to observe the action of selected stocks during these reversals. As a rule, stocks that resist deterioration when the market is under pressure tend to outperform the market during the next leg up. I especially like to see a stock give ground grudgingly on low volume, then bounce back quickly on significantly higher volume each time the market shows a modicum of strength. When the primary trend is down and short-sale candidates are being selected, stocks that remain sluggish on low volume during temporary positive market bursts, then sag quickly on increased volume when the down trend resumes, are perfect.

4) *Compatibility with current phase of the market cycle.* In the early stages of a new bull market the groups that take off first are usually consumer and housing related. As the bull matures, basic industry stocks (steels, chemicals, papers, aluminums, et cetera), energy, capital goods, and financial stocks leap ahead of the pack. The same group rotation prevails after a long consolidation phase within a primary bull market (e.g., March, 1976-December, 1977). The consumer and housing stocks should lead the market into the next upward phase after this economic "pause," then the more mature market groups should surge.

5) *Likelihood of benefiting from economic and*

political environment. Interest rates and government stimulus are the keys here. To say that interest-sensitive stocks do well when interest rates fall is a truism. Yet there is almost always a time lag when the astute investor can reap repeatedly bountiful harvests. The industries most likely to benefit from drops in short-term interest rates are the insurance companies, mortgage insurers, savings and loans, housing, and real-estate investment trusts (REIT's).

Besides providing a pep pill for overall economic expansion, government stimulus can particularly affect individual groups. Tax rebates increase spendable consumer income and can rapidly benefit consumer-related industries. Consumer spending increases retail sales and, as the retailers order to meet rising demand, manufacturers step up the pace of production to fill the orders. Democratic political regimes tend to stimulate housing; republican regimes, defense spending. A tangible example? The election of Jimmy Carter. Housing stimulation appears nearly certain, and housing issues have done well since Mr. Carter's election. They should continue strong while the economy is chugging along. After a time, groups that highlight the more mature phases of the market cycle will take over market leadership. On the other side is the defense issue. Mr. Carter promised a seven-billion-dollar cut in defense spending; defense stock issues have declined. Whether Mr. Carter actually makes the defense cuts he promised is inconsequential to the market — for the moment, the mere threat will hold the group of defense-related stocks in check. You can't fight City Hall, and who wants to! The Oval Office tells you which stocks to buy and which to avoid. In this instance it pays to listen!

6) *Active daily turnover.* Liquidity has become essential for stock investors. And rightly so. Too many investors were burned in the late '60s. Overloaded with small over-the-counter issues, they were forced to bite the bullet when they tried to unload their shares. There just weren't any bids around! A stock might have been quoted at, say, 15 bid 16 asked, but the bid was good for maybe 100 shares. Then the bid might drop to 14¼ for another hundred shares, then 13½ for the next hundred. It was not uncommon for stocks to be knocked down 10 percent or more in a single 500 or 1000 share trade! The singed pinkies of investors caught in this holocaust still smart! I think it only prudent to buy stocks with enough shares outstanding to get in and out without wild price fluctuations. For this reason I prefer to stay with New York Stock Exchange (NYSE) listed issues with average trading volumes of 10,000 shares per day or more. Why play with matches and tempt the fates?

7) *Yield provides downside prop for stock.* All other things being equal, I pick stocks within a group in which the dividend provides both income and downside protection. The problem is — all things usually aren't equal! Stocks with the greatest potential to move are often *not* those with the highest yield. In an otherwise equal decision, pick the stock on its merits, the other parameters mentioned, and consider yield only as a final consideration. Occasionally it turns out that the stock you select for best appreciation also has the best yield. One bright spot regarding dividends: corporate

payouts are increasing as companies allocate a greater percentage of their earnings to dividends. If this trend continues, and I expect it to, it will make the stock market attractive relative to other yield investments (bonds, treasury bills, et cetera) and form a solid platform, limiting downside risk and increasing potential reward.

LISTED STOCKS VS. OVER-THE-COUNTER ISSUES

As I just mentioned, I prefer listed stocks on the NYSE. As with most rules, there are a couple of notable exceptions. When an American Stock Exchange company has applied for listing on the big board and meets the other criteria mentioned, it should be considered. Nearly all such applications are accepted (otherwise the company wouldn't waste its time and money). These stocks tend to get attention and, if things are going well, they will rapidly gain sponsorship and appreciate at a quickened pace. Over-the-counter issues are another story. They are just too volatile. Rumor of the slightest problem and they nose-dive. When you are holding stocks for twelve to eighteen months, you don't need this aggravation. There is a time, however, to buy these unstable, high-risk stocks. OTC's are sponsored by various brokerage houses, many of which are small, fly-by-night outfits with relatively few clients. But occasionally an over-the-counter issue gains the sponsorship of a major brokerage house. When a brokerage firm with a big following starts touting a stock, odds are it will go up. So, *if you are one of the first* to buy it, you stand to clean up while the stock is being accumulated by the other esteemed clients of the brokerage house. When the push is over, it's time to sell *regardless of how the stock has performed.* You are gambling that the stock will go up, since it is a thin issue and is being pushed. If it does indeed appreciate, take your profits when the prop is about to be pulled; if it hasn't gone up *despite* the tout and increased buying interest, you had better cash in quickly because the bottom may drop out when the buying dries up. To play this game you must obviously be tipped off. Which brings us to a critical person — your broker.

HOW TO HANDLE BROKERS

Few realize the value of brokers. For most, a broker is merely a salesman, a guy who calls you up periodically to push this stock or that. Yet brokers can be extraordinarily helpful, and being so translates into profits for you. Before looking at how a broker can help you, let's first understand *his* needs. They are straightforward. To a broker, gross commissions are the name of the game. Gross commission is the number that appears in that little box labeled "commission" on your stock confirms. The broker receives only a percentage (usually 25–50 percent) of the gross but gross is what he and everyone else looks at. Besides feeding his family, his gross sales establish his position in the brokerage's pecking order. Each firm tabulates the annual gross commissions of its brokers. This, then, dictates such things as the broker's office accommodations, desk size, secretary (private versus use of the Medusa-like secretarial pool), underwriting positions, and status. Some houses release these gross figures to the staff to motivate them, but even if they are not officially released, everyone knows them. When a guy moves to a bigger desk in the "bull pen," it can mean only one thing — his gross is up.

"Hot" new issues are allocated to brokers based on their gross sales, not on the time they've been with the firm. In fact, *all* good things — advancements, money, status, power — flow directly from gross commissions. Needless to say, brokers will do almost anything to corral a rich source of gross. Enter the protagonist. I constantly have the gross of my brokers in mind. I keep a journal, containing a record of the monthly commissions for each of my brokers. Each time I get a stock confirm I make a journal entry. I watch the column headed "cumulative gross commission" almost as closely as I watch my profit-loss column. This way I'm right on top of what I have done for each broker.

The very best way to inflate a broker's gross is with new issues and secondaries. When a company needs to raise money, it can borrow from the bank, from investors (by selling bonds), or by selling additional stock. Many companies prefer the latter route. New stock, though representing a dilution, has no debt to be serviced and increases the number of shares in circulation. Theoretically, the greater the number of shareholders and outstanding shares, the greater the stability of the issue and the more attractive it becomes to institutions. These new stock offerings, called secondaries, are registered with the SEC and marketed by an underwriting group composed of a multitude of brokerage houses.

Secondaries are propitious for the broker-conscious investor for three reasons. First, the gross on secondaries is *two to three times* that of open-market orders! This rapidly pads the "cum gross" column. Second, selling secondaries is a real feather in your broker's homburg. Underwriting commissions provide a major source of revenues to brokerage houses. Competition for underwriting participation is keen since future participations depend upon consistently successful marketing, so each house strives to clean out its inventory on each deal. If a certain firm doesn't hold up its end and returns unmarketable shares to the "syndicate," that firm is unlikely to be considered for future issues, which results in a serious loss of revenues. So when a certain broker within the firm is consistently moving secondaries, he is likely to go far. And that's just what I want. I want my man to be a superstar, nothing less. Besides, the third advantage of buying secondaries makes them easy to swallow: they cost nothing! No commissions! The commission is paid by the company issuing the stock, usually at two to three times the regular rate. My horse gets fat at no expense. This gift giving can even be profitable. The syndicate almost always takes a short position. That is, they sell more shares than they have, covering their oversale in the aftermarket. This serves to support the offering price for several days, even in sloppy markets.

There are many companies offering their stock on the secondary market so you can be somewhat selective. *I buy secondaries only after a strong buy signal (indicators 40 and 65 percent or less), and I buy only those stocks that meet the previously outlined criteria.* On occasion I will do my broker a special favor — buy a secondary with a particularly fat commission for him even if I don't want it. Some deals are sticky, and selling a chunk of one of these results in many kudos for my burgeoning hero. I'm really not sticking my neck out *too* far. The syndicate is still intact to support the issue price. I simply turn around and immediately sell the stock through a broker outside the syndicate, eating only the sales commission — a small enough price for so large a due bill.

INTANGIBLE REWARDS

Besides providing monetary rewards to my brokers, I also supply them with other benefits. I listen to their problems. Like most businesses, selling stocks is loaded with stress. Executives are always prodding brokers toward greater sales production; there are daily foul-ups on orders, lost confirms, misplaced checks, and the like. Early in our relationship I let them know that I am interested in them and their job. I'm a willing receptacle in which they can vent their spleen. Just ventilating — verbalizing their anxieties and frustrations — works miracles. Quickly, they feel relieved and attribute their improved state of mind to our relationship — exactly what I want.

I also spend time with my broker away from the office, playing tennis, golf, squash, handball, racquet ball, and having an occasional dinner. The usual course of events is for the broker to court the client. Reversing this process is unusual, to put it mildly. But the broker laps up this treatment. It makes him feel good about himself. Thoughtful little gestures, such as giving him small gifts for Christmas, birthdays, and anniversaries produce wondrous results. People like to be remembered. It bolsters their egos, *especially* if they can see no underlying reason for the behavior. Since I am the only client doing personal favors, this treatment stands out like King Kong among the Lilliputians.

As time passes my broker advances, acquiring money, status, power, ego gratification, friendship, and goodwill. For many reasons he feels indebted to me. Only after I have sated my broker's needs, do I ask for *quid pro quo.*

RETURNING THE FAVOR

Brokers can repay me in several ways, most directly by supplying me with "hot" new issues. Near the end of a bull market, speculation runs rampant. Price-Earnings (P/E) ratios skyrocket, and investors fall all over one another, paying unbelievable prices for mere concepts. Earnings become secondary to finding that "pie in the sky." Many new companies take this opportunity to bring their stock public. These initial public offerings are generally over-subscribed and precipitously bid up to lofty levels. The real money is made by those in on the ground floor — those lucky few who snap up these deals at the *initial* offering price. The first half of 1968 typifies this new-issue-market mania "par excellence." Deals were being brought to market in droves, and most took off. It was not uncommon to see a stock, brought public at $10 per share, trade at $15 the next day, and $20 within the week! But how to get in on the ground floor? For once, brokers didn't have to make calls to sell their goods. Everyone from the Bank of America to Elmer Fudd wanted these deals. Short of printing money there was nothing better.

When giving gifts, whom do you remember? Your friends, especially the one who helped you out of those tight spots, who has fed you, and helped catapult you ahead of your colleagues. The broker now has a chance to return some of those favors, and he jumps at it. Long before each new deal was due, I let each of my brokers know my appetite. And it was hefty. As much as they could get. Everything they had. With their newly acquired status and excellent marketing record for syndicate offerings, my brokers were given generous doles of these coveted new issues and I received the lion's share — even more than the big institutions. What is five hundred shares of a ten-dollar stock to Morgan Guaranty? A pittance. But to me it meant a great deal, and I let my brokers know how much I wanted it. I got most, if not all, of their allocations, and this has continued, albeit more sporadically, to the present. And so the ledger is balanced — almost.

BEING THE FIRST TO KNOW

I ask one additional favor of my brokers: I want to be the first to hear important — therefore money-making — news. If they are going to strongly recommend a stock, especially a thin OTC stock, I want to buy it *before* the news is public. My alert brokers are right on top of these situations. Their prompt behavior is nearly always rewarded with a nice order on the spot. When the buy recommendation breaks, and the buying peaks, I sell. This maneuver is profitable 80 percent of the time and my brokers make commissions in and out. Also when a big institution is in there trying to buy 50,000 shares of a stock, one of my bloodhounds may get wind of it and share this juicy tidbit with me. More often than not, I can be in and out with a small, quick profit.

LEVERAGE

By now you're probably feeling that this scheme may work if you have a few million to play with but, unfortunately, you don't have that luxury. True it is difficult to do much for your broker if you only buy one hundred shares per year. Granted, the style I suggest is tailored more toward those with an active interest in the stock market and aggressive tendencies. But millions are not required. In January, 1968, I put $50,000 to work in a little caper that made me the *largest* individual account at *fifteen brokerage houses.* I gave them more volume than they believed I ever could and cleaned up smartly in the process. The secret was leverage. Most of you have probably bought stock on margin at one time or another. At the time of this writing the margin requirement is 50 percent. This means that if you buy, say, $20,000 of securities, your brokerage firm will lend you $10,000, or 50 percent of the total, using the stock as collateral for the loan. Using conventional margin then, my $50,000 could have purchased $100,000 in securities. But even actively traded, this amount couldn't begin to ripple the gross of fifteen of the nation's hottest brokers. So I set up a little caper to help everyone out.

I hopped on a plane and awoke next morning in Zurich. I went into an all-day conference with one of the more imaginative, ingenious financial wonder boys of the world, and together we devised a method for creating *infinite* leverage with my $50,000. I instructed each broker to deliver all the securities I purchased to my bank in Zurich. *Upon receipt,* the bank would pay for the securities. This type of arrangement, called delivery versus payment, is common for institutional use, but rarely used by individuals. It is designed to protect the buyer. If Chase Manhattan is buying, they want the actual stock certificates in hand before they part with funds. This protects the bank and its clients in the unlikely, but still possible event, that the brokerage house bellies up before making delivery. Prudent and wise. In a couple of instances it took a little persuasion, but in the end all fifteen brokerage houses agreed to my request. Then I started buying stocks in commission-rich areas as if they were going out of style. The market was strong and the calendar was laden with new issues, secondaries, and convertible bonds. My goal was to pump up the gross of all fifteen of my benefactors to the point where there would be absolutely no question about how those delectable, torrid, new deals would be allocated. I was determined to get my share, and set my sights high. In many instances I was given "special" allocations from the institutional department. My trading activity had not passed unnoticed, and my wants were clearly heard and filled.

My instructions to my Swiss banker were simple: "Sell all stocks and bonds immediately upon arrival." In addition, I called him once a week at a designated hour. Together we reviewed the list of purchases. Some we sold long *before* delivery (*i.e.*, those stocks that doubled in the first few days after issue); others we decided to hold until delivery. This latter group included the more stable secondaries and the convertible debentures.

Two factors played into my hand: an increase in transaction volume during the 1968 bull market blow-off, and the extraordinarily heavy new-issue calendar. Each new issue had to be broken down into appropriate share size for delivery, recorded, and drafted — no small task with an elephantine calendar. The *average* transit time, from time of purchase to delivery in Zurich, was seventy-five days! Ninety to one-hundred-and-twenty-day delivery was not uncommon.* This gave me the time I needed to maneuver. Many issues I sold long before arrival. All sale transactions were handled by a local Swiss-based brokerage house. Immediately upon receipt, my banker merely delivered the securities to this Swiss brokerage firm, and simultaneously picked up a check for the sale. That same day, he sent a check in payment of the delivered securities to one of the magnificent fifteen brokers. The net effect was to charge my bank account with the profit or loss. When the amount owing the American brokers exceeded $50,000 (funds available grew with my profits), my banker would simply stall for a few days until the sale transactions cleared, collect the funds, and mail them to the brokerage houses in the States. Given the turmoil in their back

* Currently, delivery times are twenty to thirty days.

offices, a few extra days made little difference. Each broker got paid reasonably promptly, and I never heard a complaint. Using this system, with a mere $50,000 I was able to buy and sell over $1,200,000 worth of securities in April, 1968, alone! The brokers were ecstatic with the business, as were their bosses. And I was quite pleased with the rewards. In a six-month period I made some two thousand trades, cornering a bundle of new issues without a hitch. The boom ended as suddenly as it began (remember the indicators hit 67 percent and 87 percent in June, 1968) and my activity dried up. But all fifteen brokers remember those glory days and will be champing at the bit next go round.

USING THE FLOAT

One of the many agreeable spin-offs of the '68 spree was free interest. By this, I mean interest paid on money that was only nominally mine. Let's say I bought $25,000 of a 6-percent convertible debenture from each of four brokers in February, 1968. From day one, I was the owner of record. Interest on bonds and convertible bonds accrues daily. If you hold a debenture ten days, you receive ten days' interest. As I mentioned, I never paid for a security until it showed up at the Swiss bank about seventy-five days after purchase. Yet interest accrued daily! This period is known as the "float." In the above example I received 6-percent interest on $100,000 for seventy-five days without putting up a penny! Twelve-hundred dollars with no investment! In my six months of active duty I earned nearly $15,000 in gratis interest alone! Mind-boggling!

NEGOTIATING COMMISSIONS

About a year ago commissions became competitive. Institutions, and individuals as well, may now negotiate their brokerage charges. Some brokerage houses have stripped their staffs to the bone, allowing them to cut as much as 50 percent off the old commission rates. The only problem is, these discount houses are usually not exactly awe inspiring. Whenever I interview these cut-rate houses, I feel I should be carrying wolfbane and a cross. One man and a secretary; sometimes just a secretary. One wonders about such small details as getting paid for sales, executions, bankruptcy, mistaken orders, and a multitude of other potential nightmares. These places are just not worth the hassle.

This does not mean, however, that I am content to sit back complacently and pay through the nose for commissions. As soon as news of the negotiable rates hit me, I met with each of the magnificent fifteen. Based on past performance, bountiful though sporadic, they knew I could be the truffle in their pâté. Preliminary bargaining rounds produced discount offers of between 10 and 25 percent. When I negotiate, I try to fathom fairness. Granted, this is a subjective concept, but I have learned that *expectation,* not reality, is the focal point of equity. My expectations were few: good executions, low margin interest rates, and occasional research reports on selected companies. I required no technical support, no opinions, no letters, no monthly strategies, and no major research. The brokers wanted a trouble-free, high-volume account, grossing approximately $20,000 in annual commissions. They knew (but I reminded them anyway) that I was capable of this production. We had the makings of a marriage. There was only one catch — the dowry. To get my business would not be easy. After all, I already had offers of 50 percent off the old rates from several people. (The only problem was, I'd have to delouse and count my money every time I left their dens.) Oh, the fifteen screamed and bleated about how I was taking the bread from their mouths, cried about their unborn babies, and complained about their families' elevated cost of living. They all "had to take my request to the highest level" and threw in all that other fodder that seems to accompany most business negotiations. But when the smoke cleared, I had struck a deal with seven of the fifteen for 40 percent off the old rates. The other eight all came in at 35 percent off. In addition my margin interest rate ranged from ½ percent *below* the prime rate to prime rate. Once I got one firm to go for 40 percent, many others quickly followed suit. Over the years I had made an impression on some of the decision makers, and they didn't want to lose a live account. Naturally, my activity has been nothing like the merry days of '68, but market conditions have not merited such heated trading. Their *expectation* nevertheless lingers and, I imagine, if they are patient, history will repeat itself. In the meantime I'm happy dealing with major, solvent firms, while saving 40 percent on commissions.

WHEN TO BUY ON MARGIN

Margin money is low-interest money borrowed from a brokerage house (at SEC controlled rates, currently 50 percent) to purchase securities, using the securities as collateral for the loan. Interest charges on margin money range from below the prime rate to about 2 percent over prime, varying with the broker. (Remember, the interest charge is often negotiable.) Deciding whether or not to buy on margin is an individual decision. Obviously, the risks are greater, as are the rewards. For myself, when the short indicators fall below 40 and 65 percent on a four-week moving average, I buy stocks. If the market then *dips*, I will buy more, often using margin to increase my position. Experience tells me that these dips are usually the final catharsis prior to a major rise, and values are at their best. I'm especially encouraged to use margin when anxiety abounds. Talk of economic collapse, depression, and worse, *provided that the specialists and members are bucking the trend,* loosens my margin purse strings. In most major moves I have found myself nearly fully margined.

WHEN TO BUY OPTIONS

The options markets have added a new dimension to security trading. They have allowed me to make money during the sometimes prolonged intervals between signals. A call option is the right to buy a given stock at a designated price at any time until the option expires. Options are traded on the Chicago Board of Options (CBOE), the American, Midwest, Philadelphia, and Pacific Stock Exchanges, and will be soon on the NYSE. Option prices are listed daily in the *Wall Street Journal.* Naturally, my option play is dictated by the indicators.

With options, you are really playing with fire. Options are volatile, so I bring another variable — interest rates — into play in order to gain some additional insurance. As you undoubtedly know, the Federal Reserve Board controls monetary policy, and therefore the economic outlook. The influence of the Fed has been particularly strong since 1968. Interest rates have varied widely of late, and moves have been rapid, all choreographed by the Fed. Low interest rates reduce the yield of fixed-income securities, encouraging a switch into equities. In addition low interest rates tend to expand the money supply and encourage capital spending by reducing the cost of money — all generally stimulating for the economy and the stock market. To decipher which way the wind is blowing at the Fed, I look at the ninety-day Treasury-bill yields. The absolute rate is not as important as the direction in which the yields are *trending*. The trend in rates is a tip-off to the Fed's course of action. I view it as bullish when the ninety-day T-bill yield * falls below its ten-month moving average ** for two consecutive months. This usually means lower interest rates and improving credit conditions. *When this key indicator coincides with below 40 and 65 percent for the short-sales indicators, I buy options.* I pick options that will expire six to nine months later to give the magic a chance to work.

The perfect condition for buying options existed in November, 1974. I bought them with dramatic results

* Ninety-Day T-bill yields are available in the *Wall Street Journal*.

** Ten-month moving average means monthly average for past ten months. As each new month is added the oldest month is dropped.

— making three to four times my investment. *I cover my option positions when the T-bill indicator turns negative,* even if the short-sale indicators are still positive (T-bill indicator rises above its ten-month moving average for two consecutive months). Options fluctuate widely and have short life-spans. They do not pay dividends. In fact, they are *penalized* by dividends. When a stock pays a dividend, the amount of the dividend is subtracted from the price of the stock. Since an option is the right to buy a stock at a fixed price, and a dividend lowers the price of that stock, a dividend reduces the value of the option. For these reasons it pays to be much more cautious with options than with stocks. I follow these rules:

1) I invest only a maximum of 15 percent of my stock-market capital in options.

2) I cover my option positions when the T-bill indicator turns negative. I do not cover my stock positions until the specialist short-sale indicator hits 60 percent, and the member short-sale indicator hits 80 percent.

WHEN TO WRITE COVERED OPTIONS

Options can be written as well as purchased. In writing an option you guarantee the buyer delivery of a stock at a given price (the striking price) at any time up until the expiration of the option, upon demand of the buyer. For this privilege the buyer pays a premium — which varies depending upon the volatility of the underlying stock but generally ranges from 5 percent to 15 percent for a six-month call — in advance.

Options can be written "covered" or "naked." A

covered option occurs when the writer of the option simultaneously purchases an equal number of shares of the stock. If the stock appreciates, the value of the option appreciates proportionately. The net effect is that the writer winds up delivering the stock to the option buyer while pocketing the premium. Since the premiums average, say, 10 percent over a six-month time interval, the writer makes an *annualized* return of 20 percent. The risk is that the stock may go down in value. The premium paid will cover the first 10 percent of the drop, but declines below that will result in losses. It pays to write covered options, then, when the market either does nothing or goes up. Once again, I rely on the short indicators to dictate timing decisions. When the *specialist short-sale indicator is between 40 and 45 percent and the member short-sale indicator is between 65 and 75 percent, I write covered options.* This is a conservative yet rewarding policy, and a good place to commit idle funds when the timing is appropriate.

WHEN TO WRITE "NAKED" OPTIONS

Writing naked options is risky business. Unlike the covered option, the call writer does *not* purchase the underlying stock. He has no stock to deliver if the stock runs up and the option is called. When this occurs, the writer is caught by the short hairs. He must buy the stock at *prevailing* prices and deliver it at the striking price, taking a blood bath in the process. The writer of naked options profits when the market goes *down*. In this event he simply pockets the premium money — a nifty profit. Due to the great risk involved should the market rally, naked options should be written only when *both* the short indicators *and* the interest-rate indicator overwhelmingly signify an imminent decline. The parameters are short indicators of 65 and 85 percent or more, *and* an *increase* in ninety-day Treasury-bill rates above its ten-month moving average for two consecutive months. Both of these bearish signals have not occurred simultaneously since the option markets were established. When this situation does crop up, I will write naked options.

WHEN TO BUY BONDS

An age-old argument rages between proponents of fixed-income securities (bonds) and stock-market fans. The bond advocate lauds the safety of his vehicle and its higher yield. Bonds tend to be far less volatile than stocks and that 9 percent, or so, rolls in every quarter. The stock enthusiast sings the praise of those big killings — 50 to 100 percent on his money in a single year — a feat impossible for the tortoise-like bond. He correctly points out that stocks also pay dividends (about 5 percent on average currently), *and* have that big capital-gain potential. So who wins, the tortoise or the hare? Both! There is a time for both and, like so many investment decisions, the relative performance is predictable.

Let's look back over the past eight years to find a clue. Using Moody's average corporate-bond indicator to follow bond movement and Standard & Poor's 400 industrial average as a broad-based stock indicator, we find that *when Moody's bond yield exceeds the S & P average dividend yield by 4 percent, bonds have out-performed equities.* Naturally, these are *average* figures and I fancy myself a pretty fair stock picker, so, when my indicators say BUY, or write covered options, I prefer the stock approach. But, when my indicators are betwixt and between, *and* when the yield difference between bonds and stocks exceeds 4 percent, I put my money in bonds. Just such an occasion arose in February, 1976. When the short indicators hit 60 and 80 percent, I liquidated my stock portfolio and covered option positions. At the same time the yield spread had jumped to an eight-year high of about 6 *percent!* I switched into bonds, averaging a whopping 16-percent return on my investment (interest and capital gains combined) from February to October. In November, 1976, the yield spread was still 4.7 percent, a very good prognosis for bonds. But at that juncture I jumped back into stocks, swayed by the incredibly low level of specialist short sales (38 percent). Bonds will still do well, and may even outperform stocks on average, but that 38-percent, October, 1976, specialist short indicator with confirmation from the bullish ninety-day T-bill trend pushed me back into stocks for the remainder of 1976. In December, 1977, the bond yield exceeded the stock dividend yield by only 3.5 percent, a negative prognosis for bonds relative to stocks.

YOUR EMOTIONS AND THE STOCK MARKET

Playing the stock market is an emotion-filled game — to put it mildly. It doesn't seem to matter how much I learn about it, I'm always scared! When I have a profit, my *emotional* reaction is to sell and take the gain; when I have a loss, my emotions would lead me to hold the stock, hoping to get even. This way lies ruin! The opposite is true. Often when my indicators are screaming buy, my emotions are screaming sell. When the indicators flash a sell signal, things usually look particularly rosy to me and my inclination is to chuck all my money into the market. What I've learned from all this is that my emotions are almost always wrong! And the stronger I feel about the direction of the stock market the greater its move *in the opposite direction!*

It has not been easy for my reason to prevail over my emotions. It's a constant struggle. Although I have disciplined myself to follow faithfully my reason, the price has been large: Fear! Even though I know through experience that I am making correct decisions, I can't escape the inevitable anxiety that comes from acting in opposition to my emotions. Yet this is the very reason why it all works! Everyone else is just as scared as I am. In fact, when everyone on Wall Street is running to the toilet every five minutes, it's usually time to buy! September, 1974: The Dow hit 570. The doom-and-gloom boys were on their soap boxes, preaching the coming of the next great depression. The prime rate was 11 percent. Corporate earnings never looked worse. Inventories were being liquidated on a grand scale. There was plague in lower Manhattan. I believed! Oh yes, I was a willing convert. There was absolutely no question in my mind. The Armageddon was at hand! But specialist short sales were 39 percent and member short sales were 62 percent. I thought my heart would stop, every cell in my body rebelled. This was insanity! But I bought stocks! In November, 1974, the T-bill indicator went positive. I took another deep breath and bought options. The rest is history.

If you follow the program I have outlined, you will undoubtedly have to contend with these same fears. They can be potent inhibitors to action. But you *must* act if you are to succeed. I can offer only two consolations to help you in your moment of need: 1) Know that your emotions will almost always be wrong. That house poised above your head by a thin thread never seems to fall; and 2) you will make money. Looking back you will laugh at yourself, wondering how you could ever have gotten your nose pushed so far out of joint. But that won't help you next time. No, the stock market is a very Zen experience: each time an investment decision has to be made it is like the first time. Even if you've seen a similar set of conditions before, you will react as if this was a new experience, and go through the same emotional turmoil. I'm afraid it's a consequence of making money in the stock market. Grin and bear it!

III

How to Invest in Real Estate

● There is no investment that has made more money for a broader segment of the population than real estate. How many of you have made money from owning your own home? The person who has lost money in a single-family residence is, indeed, a rarity. It's been hard to miss, as the market for homes has steadily appreciated. From July, 1976 to June, 1977, the median value of single-family residences in California shot up a whopping 30 percent! And this *on top of* an average appreciation of 8½ percent annually during the preceding five years. To have owned a home and lost money would have taken some doing for even the most incompetent investors. Those knowledgeable have made a killing.

This is not to say I agree with the many voices that, like a flock of newly found converts who have seen their savior unlock the doors to financial salvation, are now singing in unison the praises of real estate. On the contrary. The recent speculative boom in housing, particularly in California, scares the hell out of me. It reminds me of the new-issue craze of the 1968 stock market. Whenever three out of four people at a cocktail party are talking about the money they are making, or are about to make, in a speculative venture, the plug is about to be pulled. I am looking for a 15 percent drop in the value of single-family dwellings in California over the next twelve months, and a plateauing and consolidation of housing prices in the rest of the country. Yet I still think real estate has superb investment potential if you know what to look for. The following rules will *guarantee* your investment success:

1) Don't sell if you have to sell.
2) Don't buy if you have to buy.

The motivations of both buyer and seller are crucial ingredients in a real-estate transaction. A buyer may be motivated by a need for shelter. He may have sold his present house and must find a substitute (usually a more expensive home). He may be motivated by fear. The recent 2-percent-per-month increase in the value of California homes prodded many buyers into taking the plunge, before costs moved even higher and out of reach. Some buyers are motivated by tax consequences. For example, upon sale of a home you are given eighteen months to "step up" to a more expensive home and avoid the tax consequences of the sale. If a prospective buyer is at the end of his eighteen-month tether, he is motivated!

Some people can't stand having money around without investing it. Since real estate has stacked up favorably relative to other investments, these people feel pressured to get in there and "put their money to work." For many of these types, what they buy and what they pay take a back seat to the urgent call they feel to invest *now*. The final group, to which you will, it is hoped, belong, is motivated solely by investment potential, a potential generated by a motivated seller.

The most common motivation for sellers is the need for cash. They need money and want out of their property. Others sell because their investment has become a nuisance. If they own rental property, they may grow tired of the management and maintenance problems that constantly crop up. The better heeled they become, the less likely they are to put up with the small, but persistent, hassles. This is especially true of absentee owners. Sellers, like buyers, may be motivated by fear or tax consequences. When property appreciates, some sell to "lock in" their profits. Their motivation is fear that prices will fall and they will be forced to bear the anguish of watching handsome profits evaporate.

Taxes motivate sellers in two ways. As values rise, so do property taxes. For some the annual tax bite becomes too burdensome, so they feel they must sell. For people in the higher-income brackets, property bought for investment purposes with tax savings from write-offs starts to lose some of its luster as the write-off peters out. Rather than act as a funnel for funds from their property to the Internal Revenue Service (IRS), they choose to sell. Then there is the final class of sellers — the group that feels that a certain piece of property has met their investment parameters, and that market conditions warrant sale of the property at top dollar. Let's hope that's us.

Not feeling pressure to either buy or sell makes a tremendous difference in investment outcomes. Buying decisions stem solely from considerations of value. You can wait until a motivated seller makes you a deal you can't refuse. When selling, the decision is based on objective criteria, and you can patiently wait for that heated buyer to come along and snap up your choice bit of property *at your price.*

In December, 1974, I happened to be in Houston, Texas (for the life of me I can't remember why). A friend who dabbled in real estate told me his hair stylist needed immediate cash and had to sell his home. The housing market was far from booming at this point, the economy having suffered the worst recession in decades, and Houston, in particular, having been overbuilt. The seller feared a prolonged listing that would result in his blowing the "hot deal" that demanded quick money. He would have listed the house at $42,500, but would take $40,000 cash. I inspected the premises — not bad, as tract houses go. Nice neighborhood, four bedrooms, about 2,000 square feet of house, a good-sized lot, and a pool site. Only one hitch. Off-pink carpeting and gold-lamé (very expensive) wallpaper. (Fact!) I met with the hair stylist and told him the house had a lot going for it. It was my considered opinion, however, that in its current form it had rather a limited appeal. It just wasn't the kind of thing every cowboy would fall in love with.

Before long he got my drift and conceded it might

not put all of Houston into a swoon. That out of the way, we settled on a purchase price of $32,000, cash. He got the loot he needed and I acquired a pink-and-gold elephant. Or so it seemed, when some six months after re-listing it at $42,000, the only offer I had received was from a guy who wanted to trade for some Louisiana swampland. In addition, the house had been trashed twice by the neighborhood kids, requiring nearly $1,000 in repairs. (Unfortunately they left the carpeting and wall cover untouched, probably thinking someone else had already trashed them.) Now, if I had been in a position of *having* to sell, I clearly would have bailed out. Two things were going for me: (1) The Houston real-estate market was heating up, and (2) I did not need immediate cash, so I did a little creative financing. First, I convinced a savings and loan to finance this dream for me. They gave me $25,000 at 9 percent for twenty-five years. Then I offered the house on a lease option. For a small premium, the prospective buyer had the right to purchase the house at a fixed price at any time during the term of the option. In this case all I asked for was $1,000 down for the right to purchase this posh pad for $42,000 at any time during an eighteen-month period. In addition, the buyer would pay $450 in monthly rent for the privilege of living there.

Mercifully, within a month a cash-poor family, who could not afford the stiff down payment required to buy a house outright, scraped up the $1,000 and moved in. Now I had $26,000 in hand, was receiving $450 monthly, and had a live-in protection service to ward off the trashers. In addition, the $5,400 in annual rents represented a 16 percent return on my original investment. Things were shaping up. As fate would have it, the struggling family, New York born and raised, just couldn't "grok" the Texas mentality and fled after fourteen months, leaving me their $1,000 and the house. With some of the shekels I had received I spent $2,000 and tearfully removed the gold lamé wall coverings and pink carpets, replacing them with inexpensive, but presentable, beige carpeting and white paint. Prices were moving right along, so I relisted the refurbished version for $55,000 in August, 1976.

Once again I was confronted with a dearth of bids — four months and no action. If I had been an impatient seller, I would have missed out on more goodies. Two blocks away a fire broke out, destroying half of a neighbor's house. Since their fire-insurance policy provided up to $1,000 a month in rent, they moved into my conveniently located, and very available, sanctuary. They were able to keep their kids in the school district and the man of the family was able to preserve his three-minute commute to work. The $1,000 per month was painless, since it was the insurance company's dough. They stayed four months, vacating in April, 1977.

In early 1977, the real-estate market was really cooking on the high burner. Once again I relisted the house, this time at $59,750, and it was gobbled up for $59,000 within thirty days by someone who *had* to buy while there were still homes around he could afford.

A quick look at the mathematics tells the story (totals for the thirty-month holding time):

Costs: ($32,000
with $7,500 down payment after
refinancing with the
savings and loan.)

$32,000	Purchase Price	$59,000	Sale Price
1,000	Taxes	1,000	Option Money
500	Insurance	6,300	Rents (lease option)
2,000	Remodeling	4,000	Rents (refuge during
1,000	Trashings		repairs from
4,500	Interest to	$70,300	fire damage)
	Savings and		
	Loan		
4,500	Real-estate		
	commission		
500	Closing costs		
$46,000			
	Total profit	$24,300	

On my $7,500 investment (after refinancing with the savings and loan) I made $24,300 — a profit of over 300 percent! And all because I was able to follow those two simple rules *of not having to buy or sell.*

Another example will illustrate the flip side of this coin. An acquaintance of mine sank $125,000 into a limited partnership. A total of $450,000 was raised to build a new 116-unit apartment house on the beach in San Diego. This was in 1971. Then came the coastline initiative in California, forbidding new construction within five miles of the sea. The property appreciated, but was managed abysmally. Although occupancy was always 95 percent or more, it never seemed to generate any income. When the tax benefits began to wane, and the real-estate market softened in 1974–1975, my friend wanted out. None of the other partners wanted to sell, so he offered them his partnership interest. Knowing they had a motivated seller on their hands, the remaining partners offered him his original investment of $125,000. Since he could see little potential for the project and badly needed the money, he accepted. Eighteen months later the building was sold at the peak of the California real-estate explosion. His share of the profits would have come to $375,000! Incredible!

Real-estate investments yield to reason and patience. Unfortunately, too many decisions are based on emotion. The party that *believes* he needs the other guy more is at a disadvantage. Many deals involve high degrees of ambiguity. Real-estate negotiations are often prolonged and involve numerous contingencies. I often feel "up in the air" for what seems like an eternity, waiting for all the loose ends of a juicy proposition to be tied down. Many deals fall through. After investing such time and libido, these are especially disheartening. All I can say is, "Hang in there." If you are negotiating attractive packages, some of them are bound to fizzle. Someone else may come along, outbid you, and snap up your choice morsel. No matter. As long as each deal you close is sound, you will prosper. The trick is to recognize the good deals and pass on the others. Here's how.

WHAT TO BUY

For my money, only one class of real-estate investment makes sense — income-producing property.

Sure, it's comforting to have that choice lot in some exotic setting for your retirement twenty years from now, but as an investment it's unfortunate. Raw land ranks with whole-life insurance at the bottom of the investment barrel. It eats up your money!

Suppose you answered one of those dreamy ads offering you a little slice of heaven. They fly you up in a private plane, ply you with champagne, supply you with fishing gear, and you haul in that big trout out of your own personal stream. But you're not easily taken in. You drive a hard bargain. When the smoke clears, you have "stolen" a $15,000 lot for $10,000. And better yet, for no money down!

Let's say you hold it for five years and it appreciates 15 percent per year — $7,500 in five years. Wow! With no investment you have just pocketed a fast $7,500. Right? Wrong! There are just a few minor details you have overlooked. Interest payments on $10,000 at, say, 8 percent amount to $800 yearly, or $4,000 for the five-year period. Taxes at $200 annually suck up another $1,000. Assessments for sewer, roads, et cetera, only $200 per year, eat up another grand. That's $6,000 of your $7,500. You still have $1,500 left. But, in order to sell your land, you need help. Lacking a private plane and your own sales force, you must hire a broker. The commission on raw land is a fat 10 percent of the selling price. On $17,500, the broker's bite comes to $1,750. Then there are closing costs of another $300. You are now $550 in the hole! So, unless you are a builder or a developer, leave raw land to the suede-shoe artists and their pigeons. Save your dough for something that will make you money. The kind of investment that pencils out is income-producing property. "Income-producing" means cash in, not cash out (positive cash flow). Income property falls into three types — residential, commercial, and industrial.

RESIDENTIAL INCOME PROPERTY

Residential income property is far and away my favorite. First, it serves a basic human need, the need for shelter. Even during depressions, people *have* to live somewhere. They may cut back on purchases, businesses may fold, warehouses may sit vacant, plants may shut down, but people still need a place to live.

Residential income property may be single-family residences (houses) or multiple-family residences (apartments). Both can be superb investments if bought right. Before buying a house you plan to rent out, check the location. Find out what other houses in the area are renting for. If you can get 1 percent of the purchase price in monthly rents, you've got a viable property. For example, if you buy a house for $45,000, you need to get $450 in monthly rents. If you adhere to this rule, you will consistently make money in houses. You will have a positive cash flow on a monthly basis, *plus* appreciation down the line.

There are times, however, when the cost of houses far outstrips potential rents. In the 1976–1977 California housing boom, homes bought on speculation for $75,000 were renting for $450. This means that every month cash goes *out of pocket* to defray the expenses of the mortgage, taxes, insurance, maintenance, and the like. You simply can't cover your expenses. Those buying homes in this climate had only one purpose in mind — to turn them at a profit. In other words, speculation. To speculate is to gamble. As with gambling, unless the odds are *unquestionably* in your favor, chances are you will lose. Already, the California housing market has slowed dramatically. Some speculators, pinched by the monthly cash outflows, are beginning to become more flexible on the asking prices for their spec homes. The real-estate pages in the classified sections of California newspapers are glutted with home ads and brokers are singing, "Where Have All the Buyers Gone?" A sharp *investor* would not have heeded the speculative song of the sirens. Without his 1 percent per month in rents, he would have quickly eliminated homes in this frenzied environment from his investment checklist. In fact, he would have seen this as an ideal time to *sell* houses previously acquired for income (see "When to Sell" p. 116).

APARTMENT HOUSES

Apartment houses are slightly more difficult to evaluate. Most investors make the mistake of analyzing apartments on a multiple of gross rents. You've probably heard numbers like seven or eight times gross bandied about. These numbers have little meaning to me. What concerns me is the bottom line. Does the building make money? If so, how much? What is the likelihood of increasing profits? Note well — *profits,* not rents, is where it's at! To increase profits, I can increase income while holding expenses constant, decrease expenses while holding income constant, or both. To estimate the value of a property, I calculate the income likely to be generated under my ownership and subtract the expenses (excluding mortgage payments). This is the *net income* (before debt service) to be expected when I operate the property. To determine value, I multiply this by 10. This is my target price. Naturally, I bid *below* my target price. If this is accepted, fantastic! If not, I negotiate. But I never offer more than my target. As with stocks, I don't fall in love with a piece of property. It's only as good as its return.

"What about appreciation potential?" you ask. It's gravy. I never jump into a deal hoping for future profits. It must support itself on *current* merits. When *selling*, however, I never fail to mention appreciation potential, especially if the building has gone up in value during my tenure. Appreciation potential is a valuable lure for the motivated, emotional buyer — just the kind we are looking for when we get ready to sell.

SHOPPING CENTERS

Shopping centers are down the ladder of human needs from apartment houses. When times are good, they are teeming with shoppers and you have potential tenants knocking down your doors. When the economy slackens, chain stores draw in their tails and close their "weaker" stores. The more severe the downturn, the greater the number of weaker stores. With shopping centers it's either feast or famine. Unless you have experience with this type of real estate, stick to the relative certainty of rental units.

OFFICE BUILDINGS

Office buildings are a little more recession resistant than shopping centers. Here location is the key. And good locations tend to have exaggerated price tags. Oversupply can also become a plague. Growing areas are often overbuilt and there is a wait, sometimes quite a protracted wait, for business to catch up with building. If you find the right building in the right area at the right price, don't walk, *run* to open an escrow. Use the ten-times multiplier of the net income from operations as a guideline to purchase price. Some office buildings have single tenants on long-term net-net-net leases (that is, all expenses are paid by the lessee). This means that the occupant pays *all* expenses except debt service. A few years back you could find prime tenants willing to take net-net-net leases yielding the owner a sheltered (tax-free) cash flow of 10 percent or more. Currently, yields are down to 4 percent–5 percent or less. If this type of investment interests you, my advice is to wait for returns to rise again. These small returns aren't worth the prestige of saying that you rent to Safeway or McDonald's.

INDUSTRIAL

Industrial buildings and warehouses are subject to the ups and downs of the economic cycle and should be avoided. Only if you own your own manufacturing business should you buy rather than lease. Or, if your timing is good and you buy a distressed property, such as a bank foreclosure, at bargain prices at the end of an economic downturn, you can make a killing during the next upturn. As a rule, however, industrial property should be left for those with a thorough grasp of the market and the particular area. It's tricky business.

MINIWAREHOUSES

One type of industrial property falls outside these parameters — the miniwarehouses. These are a relatively new creation designed for transient areas. *Individual* warehouse space is rented out. This is ideal for people storing personal effects for short periods. Moving and storage companies charge exorbitant amounts for storage. Miniwarehouses are much less expensive, yet offer the owner of the facility a superb return on his investment. Because of the nature of the beast, miniwarehouses do not suffer during economic downturns. In fact, they thrive! Recessions mean job turnover, unemployment, transfers, people on the move looking for work. The miniwarehouse is an excellent repository for their goods during these periods of transition. Until these dandy little money-makers become overbuilt, they should be strongly considered as a lucrative source of income.

WHERE TO BUY

The areas that offer the highest potential return on investment are rapidly growing middle-income areas. I avoid low-end and high-end areas. Low-end areas have management and maintenance problems. Tenants are always strapped for money and rent collection is a constant headache. Buildings in high-end areas usually have small yields. You pay for the prestige. Unfortunately, prestige doesn't spend very well. Although you may find an occasional pearl on Park Place, the high-rent district is generally not worth the looking. Middle America, Chevy country, that's what we're looking for. Not the type of building you might ohh and ahh over every time you pass; rather that benign, mediocre-looking building you've passed hundreds of times without noticing. Nothing special. Just functional, low-maintenance housing. It's what I call bread-and-butter housing. It churns out the bucks month after month with a minimal amount of aggravation. Interestingly enough, it also appreciates. Percentagewise, it appreciates more than those ritzy, marble-columned, Beverly Hills Taj Mahals. Your sale may not hit the society pages, but it will hit the ledgers of your bank account. When buying homes for income, the same formula applies. The $50,000–$65,000 range is optimal (as long as you can get the $500–$650 you need in monthly rents).

HOW TO FIND PROPERTY

The most frequent question I am asked is: "Where do you find good property?" The answer is: "Everywhere I look." But I have to look. I don't mean I systematically scan neighborhoods seeking out buildings, but I am *always* in the market for good deals. I let all my acquaintances know I am interested in real-estate investments. I have brokers in no less than ten areas of the country on the *qui vive* for property that meets certain criteria.

When I travel, I'm vocal about my interest in property. Prime properties pop up in the most unexpected ways. About a year ago I was at a cocktail party in Phoenix. Phoenix is one of those growing sunbelt areas that meets my investment criteria. At the party was a banker I had never met before. We hit it off pretty well and spent most of the evening talking about interest rates, the stock market, housing starts, and the like. True to my policy, I apprised him of my interest in investing in real estate. Before the evening ended, he confided in me that he had a problem. He had purchased thirty-six units and through an "oversight" his bank was the holder of the first mortgage. Being a high-ranking bank officer, this might be construed as a conflict of interest. He had bought the property "right," "very right," in fact, and could sell it at an attractive price and still come out whole. He had been planning to sell it for some time now, but had gotten so bogged down with paper work that time had slipped by without his taking any action. The problem was becoming particularly thorny because the bank auditors were due in three days and were likely to discover this cozy little deal that would be "embarrassing" for him. Bluntly put, his ass was in a sling! I told him I'd be in his office at nine o'clock next morning.

Our brief meeting next day was followed by a physical inspection of the property. We struck a deal at 7.5 times the current net income from operations! He was off the hook and I had a real prize. The building generated a 27-percent cash flow the first year!

Ah, I know what you're thinking. "This is a rarity," you say. "A once-in-a-lifetime occurrence." Not so! Although the form may be different, circumstances similar to these occur several times each year. You have to recognize them and move quickly.

Three short months after saving the Phoenix banker's neck, I was chatting about real estate with my hair stylist. He handles both men and women and told me he had just finished doing a lady who wanted to sell a seven-unit building she had owned for thirty years. I had him call her and arrange for a meeting that afternoon. She was a delightful spry Irishwoman in her mid-seventies. As much as she loved the building, she was getting on, and it was just too much for her to manage. Although over forty years old, the building was in exceptional condition inside and out. It had been totally renovated five years before and had been impeccably maintained. The lady obviously had great pride in ownership. When she told me what she wanted for it, I blanched. At the price she quoted, it would have been a good buy ten years ago. No dickering here. I wrote out a deposit check on the spot and drove her over to the nearest title company to open an escrow.

Then there are the absentee owners — the investors who buy a building and don't take another look at it for five years. I've had these kinds of investors jump at offers far below market. Why? They see what looks like a nice fat profit. In truth, it *was* a nice fat profit. Just not as plump as it might have been had they done their homework.

There are many reasons why people sell income units. Some have been milked and have been allowed to deteriorate. A run-down building in a good area is a prime target for purchase. There is a reason why the owner is not maintaining it. Maybe he doesn't want to spend the money. Perhaps it's too much trouble. Sometimes he doesn't even know his formerly nice building has fallen apart. Whatever the reason, a run-down building is a problem building for the owner. Odds are the tenants are unhappy and vacancies are running high. Rents have not kept up with the nicer-looking buildings in the area. I evaluate the going rents for the area, calculate the cost of rehabilitating the building, dig up the name of the owner from the county offices, and make an offer. You'll be amazed! This is an extremely productive procedure. In my experience, about one in four is willing to sell at a reasonable price. I buy the building, fix it up, raise the rents, and hold it until a rising real-estate market develops.

There are many sources of good real estate. Let the word out that you are an investor. If you hear about projects that are too large for you alone, talk with your friends. You may be able to form a partnership and even get paid for organizing it. (Take a piece of the deal with no investment as an organizational fee.) The more people who know you're in the market, the higher your probability of hearing about sweet deals. Talk it up.

WHEN TO SELL

When the purchase criteria outlined here are rigorously followed, the properties take care of themselves, even during hard times. You will have enough flexibility to lower rents if you have to, and still come out whole. In the meantime your equity (the amount paid toward principal on your mortgage) builds up. Then, when good times roll around again — and despite the many harbingers of doom, they *do* roll around — you can raise rents and sell. The hotter the real-estate market, the more people clamor about real estate being the last bastion of financial security, the more likely I am to be a seller.

People ask me, "How can you sell a beautiful property like that?"

The answer is simple. If others are willing to pay me substantially more than I feel the building is worth, I can be persuaded to part with choice properties.

How much is enough? That's a more difficult question. In general, if I can get fifteen times my net operating income, I can be talked into selling.

During the 1977 California real-estate boom, income properties soared over the rainbow. One building I sold (to a major insurance company, no less) at twenty times net operating income. The buyer had a *negative* cash flow of over 20 percent! Put another way, the new owner would have to raise rents by 25 percent to break even. Madness!

Negative cash flows have become common in the California market. A client recently showed me an eight-million-dollar deal with a 4-percent cash flow and was bursting with enthusiasm over his rare find. Absurd! I pass. This is the *perfect* market to sell into. I have advised all my clients with California holdings to liquidate or, better still, to trade into *income-producing* properties in other areas. Amazingly enough, I have met staunch resistance. California investors are convinced that this is just the tip of the real-estate iceberg, that property values will continue to soar 20 percent–30 percent annually. When I ask why, they look at me as if I were the Mad Hatter. "Don't you see what's happening? People have nowhere to stick their money but in real estate. And that big freeze they had this winter in the East is driving the people to California in droves. Prices have to keep going up." I've had to make hard presentations to control these wild-eyed investors.

To begin with, buyers are willing to bid up prices to the point of negative cash flows. This situation has *never* existed before in the entire history of the real-estate market. Sure, it's possibly the beginning of a new trend, but reason leads me to believe this is just an aberration. Let's face it, why would someone, presumably with his head screwed on properly, buy a building that was losing money? Only two reasons make sense. First, he plans either to raise rents or to cut expenses enough to put the building in the black. Or else he is betting on the come, hoping that the building will appreciate *still* further and that he will find someone willing to run even a larger deficit for the privilege of ownership. It's the greater-fool theory.

Several centuries ago the same situation existed with tulip bulbs. Frenzied buyers bid up the price of the bulbs of rare species of tulips. Speculators, with as much interest in tulips as gout, bought bulbs, only to turn around and resell them at a higher price to another speculator. Some bulbs went for thousands when the fever reached its peak. Then, suddenly, the market dried up. Buyers vanished. Speculators were left holding the bulbs with only true flower lovers willing to pay twenty-five dollars or so for a prize bulb. Whoops!

In the end *all* markets — be it stocks, real estate, gold, or tulips — come into equilibrium with economic factors. If an investment has questionable intrinsic value, *eventually* investors wise up. I think the perfect time to sell is when everyone else desires to buy. I don't want to squeeze out the last dollar. Let some tulip buyer take his best shot.

Look what can be done during times like these. A group of my clients bought an apartment house in Malibu, California, in 1970. We paid ten times our projected net income from operations. Our purchase price was $1,500,000 with $300,000 down. The building threw off a net cash flow of 8 percent ($24,000) annually. Then we began to raise rents. By 1976 our yearly cash flow was up to 15 percent ($45,000) based on our original investment. In addition we had built up $60,000 in equity on our mortgage. Then came the stampede of would-be buyers. We were plagued by real-estate brokers and barraged with offers. Finally someone made us an offer we couldn't refuse. The offer was for a cool $3,000,000 with new financing. We got cash and didn't have to carry back any paper (second mortgage). After costs and com-

missions, we netted $1,200,000 on our $300,000 investment *plus* the tidy annual amounts we had drawn. Not
bad so far, but the government would take its toll. The
prospect of giving 35 percent of this score to Uncle was
appalling, so we prolonged the closing of escrow and I
went off to find a more reasonably valued substitute.

Within thirty days I had found just what we were
looking for. In Houston, Texas, I found a 176-unit building for sale for $4,200,000. The net income from opera-
tions was $416,000 a year. I offered $4,000,000 and we
settled at $4,100,000, a shade under ten times net oper-
ating income. Our net cash flow was $115,000 a year,
over *double* the cash flow of our Malibu property.

Doubling our income was wonderful. What was
even nicer was that in the process of increasing our annual return, we avoided paying any income taxes on our
profits! In escrow, we had the buyers of our Malibu
property first buy the Houston property; then, before
the ink was dry, they exchanged this property for our
Malibu property. This is called a "tax-deferred exchange" (see below).

All in all our group came out with a much larger,
more productive property at the expense of the tulip
buyers. They may also make money, but which would
you rather have, the prestige of Malibu or an additional
$70,000 a year in Houston?

The same principle applies to rehabilitated properties. After fixing them up and raising rents, hold them
until the real-estate market begins to simmer. Then
trade up.

TAX-DEFERRED EXCHANGES

Normally, when you sell a building (or anything else, for that matter) at a profit, you must share the profits with your partner — your friendly Uncle. The IRS is your silent partner in business and in investments. You may not feel that Uncle carries his load, but he tends to take his cut anyway. There are statutes in the IRS code, however, that allow you, under certain conditions, to defer the government's share. If you are clever, you can extend this involuntary tithing indefinitely. Sections 1231 and 1031 of the IRS code deal with nontaxable exchanges. In summary, they say the following:

If you own a property *held for investment* (this is critical) and exchange it for another investment property of equal or greater value, there are no tax consequences. That's right — none! No tax on the gain; no recapture on the depreciation you have taken over the years. Simple as that. Disadvantages? Your basis (book value) in the new building is lowered because of the depreciation you took on the old building, so your depreciation on the new building is less than it would have been in an outright purchase. But this is a small enough price to pay and has no real consequences. Because your new project will generally be more expensive (as in the actual example I gave — Houston for Malibu), there is still enough depreciation to shelter a large portion of the income.

The significance of this section of the tax code is major. It means that as long as you keep trading up, you *never* have to pay any taxes. You can build your estate keeping *all* the money you make to plow into the next deal. If the amount gets too high, you can trade one big building for two smaller ones. Or you can trade five small ones for one large one. The possibilities are vast.

You don't have to go out and find someone with a building of equal or greater value who wants to trade. Let's say you have a buyer for your building and have selected a larger property for a trade. The seller of the larger property wants to cash out. All you have to do is have the buyer of your property at the closing of escrow sign a few documents. First he signs to buy the property you want to trade into; then he signs exchanging this property for the one you own. The result is that everyone gets what he wants. Yes, this is legal. I've done it. It's okay with the IRS. It's beautiful!

CREATIVE FINANCING

When you buy a home or a building, you put 29 percent down and finance the balance with a savings and loan, bank, or with the owner. This is the standard rhetoric for buying property. It's just that — rhetoric! There are no standards for down payments, interest rates, terms of notes, or anything else in real estate. The whole ball of wax is negotiable. Aha! Magic word. Negotiable. By now you know a good deal about how to negotiate. There is no area more appropriate for your newfound skills than real estate.

For openers you will be dealing with people generally less sophisticated than yourself. This includes brokers. You'll be surprised how backward brokers can be. That's where that "29-percent-down" stuff originates! Most brokers are salesmen, pure and simple.

They are not knowledgeable when it comes to the fine points of exchanges and creative financing. So get your facts straight, figure out the best way for *you* to go, and forge ahead, using your arsenal of negotiating skills. Show the seller (or buyer) and the broker how you are filling *their* needs. You'll be amazed at what you can pull off.

There are two rules that apply to financing income property:

Rule 1 — Never borrow *more* than the building will support.

Rule 2 — Never borrow *less* than the building will support.

Naturally, the seller will want a hefty down payment, probably 29 percent. What the seller wants, and what he gets, are two different things. Most buyers will dicker about the purchase price because they know that asking prices are usually inflated, but they tend to accept passively the downstroke and terms. To tackle this virgin territory all you need is a little knowledge to go with your negotiating skills.

THE SECOND MORTGAGE

The simplest way to increase the financing on a deal and reduce the amount of cash out of pocket is to have the seller carry back a second deed of trust. Obtain a first deed of trust for 75 to 80 percent of the cost of the property from a savings and loan, then have the seller carry a second mortgage for 10- to 15-percent of the purchase price. This reduces your cash down payments to 10 percent of the purchase price, or one-third as much cash out of pocket when compared to the standard 29 percent down.

Arguments encouraging the seller to proceed along these paths include:

1) If he has faith in the building, he shouldn't be afraid to finance part of it. In the worst case (if you defaulted on the second), he would have the building back and keep your down payment.

2) Find out what he plans to do with the cash. If he is planning to stick it in a savings account or buy certificates of deposit, point out that he can get more interest by lending the funds to you with the building as collateral (second mortgage). At best he will receive, say, 7½ percent from the bank. You'll pay him 8 percent. If he perceives that this issue may make or break the deal, he may see his way clear to invest in his property rather than the savings and loan.

3) Appeal to the seller's ego. Point out the magnitude of his knowledge of the building and surrounding area, and how much you respect his opinions. Tell him you really need his help and value his insights. Having a second assures a continuing relationship.

4) Hold out the carrot of future deals. If this project works out, you may very well want to buy other properties. By his taking a second and establishing an ongoing relationship, he will form a foundation for other projects. What you *don't* tell him is that this format establishes a precedent for future transactions. Using the

promise of subsequent deals as a lever, I was about to convince an elderly property owner to take a second on a smallish project I bought from him. It worked out swimmingly, so I pressed him for more. I wound up buying three additional buildings from him, and *all* with twenty-five-year, 8-percent second mortgages on them. My down payment varied from 8 percent to 10 percent of the purchase price. By convincing this seller that a second was a good way for him to go on the first project, I paved the way for using the same format on the other three buildings, substantially increasing my leverage.

THE WRAP-AROUND MORTGAGE

The wrap-around, or all-inclusive, mortgage is as nifty a financing ploy as you will find. It's another one of those goodies where everyone wins. Well, almost everyone. The only one who may be a bit chagrined by this caper is the savings and loan officer, but he will go along with it, albeit grudgingly.

Mortgage rates vary from time to time, depending upon the dynamics of supply and demand. The real-estate market has its slack times, and when business is off, builders and owners can't meet their payments, and the savings and loans wind up with unwanted properties. This results in hot collars, sweaty palms, and a melting of the smile usually frozen on the lips of our friendly savings and loan officer. The last thing he wants to be is a landlord. He wants to rent money, not buildings. During these periods of anxiety, savings and loans are likely to wheel and deal as they frantically scramble to get out of the real-estate business and back into the money business. They are motivated to make loans at very low interest rates with excellent terms. When the real-estate market improves, these low-rate, long-term loans lose their glitter, as the savings and loans greedily push up rates and tighten terms. Those projects that looked so shaky when times were bad become solid when the real-estate market percolates. The savings and loans' problems change too. Instead of begging people to take deals off their hands, they are inundated with loan applications. The problem is no longer disposing of property — they want to retire their low-interest loans. And guess which loans head their list? The very same ones they were so anxious to make a short while back. In a booming market those low-interest loans look bad on the books, especially when there would be no problem putting the money back out at, say, 9½ percent instead of at 6½ percent!

Savings and loans have a built-in escape clause. In the loan agreement they include a cleverly worded paragraph called an acceleration clause. This bit of banking wizardry calls for a loan to become due and payable immediately if the building is sold. The loan cannot be assumed by a third party. In other words, if the building is sold, the loan gets paid. That's the intent. Here, the savings and loan is relying on human nature. Its logic is faultless. If a guy picks up a distressed building at bargain prices during hard times, he is likely to want to cash in his chips when times are good. He'll make a killing, and in the process of selling he will, in passing, get the savings and loan out of that horrible low-interest, long-term obligation it made under duress. When market forces are at work, the natural process gets the savings and loans off the hook, so long as there is no tampering with the natural, cyclical flow of events. We're about to tamper.

I feel no compulsion whatever to let the savings and loan slip out from under those lean loans. They may be unappetizing to the savings and loan, but to a property buyer they are Grade-AAA choice! There is a major difference between a 6½-percent, forty-year loan with thirty-five years remaining and a new 9½-percent, twenty-five-year loan. That low-interest loan can really make a deal. To give it up lightly, and blindly go out seeking new financing, is an appalling notion. But how to get around the acceleration clause? Here we get creative.

To illustrate this point, here's a concrete example. Two years ago I was interested in purchasing a fourteen-unit building for $150,000. The building had been a problem in the past, which probably explains the 6¾-percent, thirty-five-year, $110,000 note enjoyed by the seller. The note had twenty-nine years remaining. I told the seller I would buy his building *at the listed price* of $150,000. I would give him $15,000 down and *he* would carry back a *first* mortgage for $135,000 at 7¼ percent for twenty-nine years on a contract of sale. This mortgage is an all-inclusive one, meaning that all other outstanding mortgages, namely, that tasty 6¾-percent note from the savings and loan, remain the obligation of the seller. A contract was drawn up clearly stating the obligations of buyer and seller. Title would not pass until all the provisions of the contract were met (see next heading). This little maneuver will keep the savings and loan on the hook. The loan officer may thrash like a marlin, but on the hook he will stay until the loan expires.

Savings and loans, needless to say, have taken issue with these tactics. In California, notorious for furious real-estate activity, Lassen Savings and Loan decided to test the legality of this type of caper. They accelerated an underlying loan, claiming that this financing gimmick was really an assumption of the loan by a third party, giving them the right to accelerate and call the loan. The case went to the California Supreme Court. The decision marked a sorry day for the savings and loans. The Court ruled (Tucker versus Lassen Savings & Loan) that a contract of sale is *not* an assumption. They stated that the position of the lender (the savings and loan) is in no way jeopardized by the contract of sale. In fact, it is strengthened. This decision paved the way for contracts of sale and wrap-around mortgages, providing a great deal of leeway for buyers and sellers at the expense of the savings and loan companies. As for the status in other states, check with your attorney. To my knowledge no state has upheld the savings-and-loan position. In most states there probably has been no judicial action on this issue. But savings and loans in states other than California will think twice before accelerating loans wrapped in contracts of sale. For one thing, they are quite aware of the California ruling, and probably don't want to test it. They prefer to just keep things as hush-hush as possible in hopes that the poor loans in their portfolio get paid off. Publicity only arouses public attention to the existence of this financing device, and the savings and loan officers I've talked to prefer to keep the whole issue low key and out of the courts and newspapers. They are willing to be had by a few sophisticated investors, so as not to wake up the dead. My advice is to exploit this situation whenever possible.

CONTRACT OF SALE

A contract of sale is an agreement between buyer and seller. The buyer agrees to pay the seller a fixed monthly or annual amount over the term of the contract. The seller keeps title to the property until all the terms and provisions of the contract are met. Only then does title pass. In the meantime, however, the buyer enjoys all the benefits of the property, including the cash flow and write-offs. The buyer also has the right to sell the property, subject to the provisions of the contract. The buyer may opt to write another contract with a new buyer, including the provisions of the old contract as conditions of the new contract.

Contracts of sale are often combined with wrap-around mortgages, as in the example described under the preceding heading. This combination is dynamite! Let's go back to the example and look at it from the standpoint of both buyer and seller. The seller got his *full* asking price of $150,000, more than he had anticipated. The $15,000 downstroke might have been less than ideal, but the wrap-around and purchase price made up for it. Since he is getting 7¼ percent but paying out 6¾ percent on $110,000, he pockets $550 every year for the next twenty-nine years, or a total of about $16,000 — on the savings and loan's money! Pretty sweet! In addition — because he is receiving his money in installments, his tax consequences from the sale are spread out over a twenty-nine-year time span, minimizing his tax burden. All in all, a very good deal for the seller.

And equally appetizing for the buyer — 10 percent down, a 7¼-percent, twenty-nine-year mortgage. Small down payment, low interest rate, and a long-term mortgage. What more could one desire?

When the buyer is ready to sell a few years down the line, the savings and loan *still* has no escape. If he's smart the owner will "wrap the wrap." In other words, he will create a new contract of sale and wrap-around mortgage for the new buyer. Say, he sells in three years for $190,000. He takes $30,000 down and creates an all-time inclusive note for $160,000 at 8 percent for twenty-six years. The seller is obligated for the $135,000, 7¼-percent outstanding note, but this is well covered by the new $160,000, 8-percent note. The seller picks up ¾-percent interest on the $135,000, or about $1,000 per year, for twenty-six years — a cool twenty-six grand! As you can see, this financing ploy allows the participants in real-estate projects to cut up the interest booty that would normally go to the savings and loan. The savings and loan is saddled with a loan it would rather not have for the duration. It has no out. For once, the little guys get the marrow bone!

REFINANCING EXISTING LOANS

An alternative to the wrap-around mortgage is refinancing an existing low-interest loan with the savings and loan. Suppose there is a 6-percent first mortgage with twenty years remaining on a building I'm interested in buying, and the seller absolutely insists on being cashed out. Negotiations with the lender are in order. The fact that this is not a prize loan is no secret to him. His opinion of the loan will be further reduced if the building is in disrepair. The prospect of writing a new loan at, say, 8 percent for twenty-five years should interest him. There is a big difference between a 6-percent loan and an 8-percent loan. As part of the package, I have found that I can often increase the amount of the loan to cover the planned improvements. And all at 8 percent. Good for the savings and loan, good for the seller (he gets his cash), and good for me. Everyone is happy.

NEGOTIATING WITH SAVINGS AND LOANS

Many savings and loan officers would have you believe that all their loans are "standard." Rubbish! They are only standard if you passively go along with the program and sign on the dotted line. Most buyers are so honored by the opportunity to obtain a loan that they blindly sign whatever is put before them. If you are to negotiate favorable loans, you must not stand at the altar, quaking with fear before the graying, authoritarian god that controls the purse strings. The savings and loan uses this power base to get you to swallow unpalatable agreements filled with clauses bordering on larceny. If you're not careful, it will charge you for the privilege of getting the loan (loan fees), not allow you to assign the loan to anyone else, and even nick you for repaying the loan early. They literally get you coming and going!

The best way to combat this is to deal from strength. Instead of bowing and scraping, project an air of confidence. Present yourself and the project in such a way that the savings and loan *wants* the loan. The more they want it, the more concessions they are likely to make. To get their stony representatives to start salivating is no easy task. It takes some work. When in the market for money, prepare a formal presentation. This includes the following:

1) A *description* of the property. Where it is located; a description of the surrounding area; amenities, such as shopping conveniences, availability of transportation, schools, parks, et cetera. Also include an accurate legal description of the property.

2) A *market survey* of the area. How does your prospective building compare with other properties in the area? Compare general condition of the property with others — rental schedules, improvements (swimming pools, gardens, et cetera). Include pictures of the building and others in the area.

3) *Improvements.* Detail planned improvements, including costs. Note how your building will compare with others in the area after improvements. Include pic-

tures where pertinent. Analyze the effects of these improvements on rental schedules, occupancy rates, and value of the building after improvements.

4) *Operating statements* — Include a current operating statement (present owners). Show how this statement will change under your ownership: (a) before improvements and (b) after improvements.

5) *Preliminary title report* — Have your attorney or title company pull a preliminary title report. This will show if there are any liens, loans, or other encumbrances against the property.

6) *Appraisal* — On larger properties try to include an appraisal from members of the American Institute of Real Estate Appraisers (M.A.I.) * especially if the appraised value is substantially higher than the purchase price. M.A.I. is a very prestigious title. Savings and loans and banks are impressed when they see this as part of the package. Only one hitch. They are expensive — about $1,000 to $2,000 depending on the size of the building. When dealing with large projects, it's worth getting the M.A.I. appraisal, especially if the deal is tied up in escrow with no escape clauses for the seller. This can be the most significant part of the presentation. If the savings and loan feels there is a tidy cushion between the purchase price and market value, it means additional protection for their loan, a most desirable situation. But make *absolutely* certain the deal is tied up before you apprise the bank of the building's value.

* M.A.I. appraisers are the ultimate in the business. Their decisions are accepted by all lending institutions.

About a year ago I learned a painful lesson. I negotiated an incredible deal — a sixty-unit apartment in a *choice* location for $650,000. The units were *not* on the market. I knew the owner personally and negotiated the deal pending adequate financing. The owner was a semi-recluse and did not want to bother setting up an escrow until the deal was done. He suggested I arrange the financing, then we could close in "one shot." I got an M.A.I. appraisal. The value of the building was a staggering $950,000! I put together a lovely presentation and marched into the leading local savings and loan, brimming with confidence. The loan officer knew the building well — too well. A week later he approved the loan. Happily, I pranced back to the seller, the deal done. A rude shock awaited me. It seemed that during the week another offer had mysteriously materialized — for $850,000! The seller was duly apologetic, but felt compelled to accept the new offer. Later I found out the building was financed by the same savings and loan I had visited. Coincidence? Perhaps. But I don't believe it. Not only did I lose the building, but I was out $1,200 for the appraisal. Now I tie my projects down before I start shopping loans. No exceptions!

7) *Personal Information* — Here I include my qualifications as an owner. Other properties owned. My track record. I also include a personal financial statement. I know they will ask me for it anyway, so I may as well take the lead. It's an integral part of dealing from strength.

8) *Loan Presentation* — The last step is asking for the loan. Prospective buyers usually ask lending in-

stitutions what they are willing to lend on a property. I state the conditions I am willing to accept. This usually includes a fair interest rate, currently around 9 percent–9¼ percent, *without* loan fees. It also *always* includes the right to assign the loan *once,* without charge, and the right to pay it off without penalty. The term is never less than twenty-five years. Skeptical? You'll be surprised. If the package looks good, the loan will get priority treatment, and the savings and loan will accept your terms. At the time of this writing the savings and loans are awash with funds, and they are looking for prime loans. Give them what they want! They are willing to bend a little for "quality" loans.

It helps to deal with one of the head muckamucks at the savings and loan, someone who can make decisions without "going to committee." If you have a contact at the savings and loan, ask to meet the president or executive vice-president. If you are granted an audience, explain that you are a real-estate investor and show him some of your exploits. Tell him that in the future you may need someone of his stature to give you quick decisions on certain properties. You'd like to be able to call him directly to discuss your needs.

If you are going in cold, try to get the name of the chief. If the savings and loan is public, your broker can glean the president's name from an annual report. If you are dealing with a branch office, charm the receptionist into revealing the identity of the boss. Then request a meeting. If you are asked the nature of your business, say it concerns a "significant" real-estate project that requires a personal explanation. No, you can't send in any information. Insist on a personal meeting. Then make sure everything is in order when you make your presentation. Once the officer finances one property, you've got an open door on subsequent deals. Make a good first impression. Here's how.

HOW TO RELATE TO LENDING OFFICERS

Efficiency, prudence, thoroughness. These are buzz words for the savings-and-loan officer. It's this image that you must project to get good loans. These qualities should be packaged with your other negotiating skills — "I" language, active listening, et cetera. Your formal presentation will go a long way toward convincing your loan officer that you possess the characteristics he seeks. Take him through it page by page, pointing out salient features.

When I am at a loan officer's desk, I'm all business. With modulated voice, I painstakingly carry him through my presentation. All bases are covered. He feels secure with the step-by-step planning that has been done. Then *I* take *him* to lunch. At lunch the talk is lighter, more cordial. In the course of the discussions, I always bring up prior successes and other projects I'm currently investigating. He sees the promise of a profitable ongoing relationship. Trouble-free loans to people who know what they are doing — that's what he is looking for. I make it so that he needn't look too far. This initial luncheon helps round out his opinion of me. I usually get the loan I have requested with little or no compromise.

I continue to make periodic calls on my loan officer, even if I have no new business to discuss. An occasional lunch to apprise him of the status of *his* project is greatly appreciated. He feels I have a personal interest in him and appreciates the thoughtfulness. When I do present him with the next project, he is comfortable with me and ready to make the new loan.

Once you get next to a few loan officers in different localities, you can use *their* contacts in other areas. Often they have met other loan officers from various parts of the country at meetings, conventions, and the like. When I am looking for money in virgin territory, the first people I contact are the people I know. More often than not they refer me to a ranking officer in the new area.

Loan officers are valuable assets, I treat them with respect, and fill their needs as best I can. The favor is returned, in spades!

HOW TO RELATE TO APPRAISERS

Appraisers are an important part of my real-estate team. Most investors view appraisers as the enemy. This is a self-defeating approach. I court appraisers. That's right, more lunches. These are especially appreciated, because appraisers are rarely showered with attention. When it's time to get down to business, I go with them to examine the property. There are three basic models used for appraisals.

1) *Replacement* model — What would it cost to rebuild the existing structure at today's prices?

2) *Market-value model* — What have comparable buildings sold for recently?

3) *Income model* — What is the value of the building based on the income it produces?

Appraisers are a very honest breed. To get the lofty M.A.I. credential, they must be beyond suspicion. This does not mean, however, that they cannot be directed and aided in their pursuits. For example, if comparable sales have recently been made that would cast an appraisal in a favorable light, I tactfully point these out. An appraiser can easily verify them. It saves him time and me money. Naturally, I select those sales most favorable to my cause. If improvements are to be made and rents raised, I encourage the appraiser to project the value *after* improvements. For documentation, I lead him to selected buildings sporting similar improvements and getting full rents. I bypass those buildings where I feel the rents are too low.

If both comparable sales and income models leave something to be desired, I bring up the subject of replacement value. Properly curried appraisers usually get the drift and lean toward this model of evaluation. Time spent with appraisers has a high rate of return!

MANAGING PROPERTIES

Selecting a resident manager — *the* resident manager — is crucial to the success of a building. A good manager will take away your headaches; a bad one will bust you.

My best managers are middle-aged couples. The woman usually works out front, showing the apartments, keeping them rented, ordering supplies, controlling advertising, doing the books, et cetera. The man putters around, helping with small maintenance problems such as leaky faucets and clogged toilets. Most managers are eager to supplement their income by cleaning vacated units. I will *not* let them get involved, however, in major repairs, such as painting, wallpapering, or carpeting, no matter how much interest they show. This is clearly a conflict of interest to my mind. They wind up playing fix-it instead of managing. When the managers are being paid for painting, apartments tend to need paint much more often. Best to leave the painting to the painters and the managing to the managers.

The best place to find a resident manager is in an existing building. I "shop" other apartments in the area, representing myself as a prospective tenant. When I find a good-looking building and get a proper sales presentation from a snappy woman of a certain age, my tentacles quiver. I make several return trips, asking plenty of questions. If she continues to pan out, I invite her (and her husband) to lunch. At lunch I find out how much they are making, what their duties are, how long they've been managing, as well as other pertinent information. If pleased, I offer them a job on the spot. When there are no good managers to steal, I advertise in the local paper for well-groomed, energetic people with high interpersonal competence. If they can deal with people, they can be trained to manage.

COMPENSATING RESIDENT MANAGERS

Resident managers are usually paid embarrassingly little. Yet the right ones can save an owner thousands. I like to give them a base salary plus a percentage of the profits beyond a certain point. The starting point is the profit schedule I projected in my presentation to the lender. If this target is met, the building is a guaranteed winner. Beyond this goal, I dole out a generous 20 percent of the profits to the resident manager. As far as I'm concerned, my 80 percent is pure gravy. If their management talents raise profits beyond my projections, they are entitled to a hefty slice. Giving them a percentage of the profits, rather than the gross income, encourages them to control expenses. I've been amazed at what some of them have been able to accomplish. They do very well for themselves, and I'm delighted.

PROFESSIONAL MANAGEMENT

An outside company specializing in property management is often warranted for large buildings with absentee owners. When selecting a firm, visit properties they currently manage. Talk with the resident managers in these projects. Get feedback from the tenants in these buildings. After checking out three or four projects, you will get a feel for the competence of the management company. If you get a good one, all you should have to do is spend your money.

OTHER PROFESSIONAL HELP

A solid real-estate attorney and an excellent accountant are well worth their cost. You want a team that can save you as many tax dollars as possible without creating problems for you. Good men know what will fly with the IRS and maximize your tax savings while protecting your flanks. They deserve to be well compensated.

RAISING RENTS

When should rents be raised? As often as possible. I have never seen more financial complacency than in the area of rents. Many property owners raise rents only when their costs increase. Tax increases are the most common stimuli for rent increases. Apologetically, the owner passes on his increased costs to his tenants and is flabbergasted when no one moves out. Why should they? The rental market is way behind the rest of real estate. Although home values have zoomed in the past several years, rents have only inched upward. In many buildings, the rents are less than the market will bear. The owners are making money at the current rent schedule and don't want to "rock the boat." I have bought some buildings where I could raise rents by 50 percent!

When raising rents, I don't plunge ahead as soon as I leave the title company. One can live without an uprising among the existing tenants. For new tenants, however, there are new rates and these are often substantially higher. The old tenants see apartments renting at elevated prices. People are actually paying these dizzy sums! Madness, they think. Then more strange things begin to happen. There is a new manager, a likable, lively sort who seems to know what she's doing. The old tenants are getting service — professional service. A landscape architect arrives, and lovely touches spring up overnight. A fresh coat of high-quality paint freshens up the exterior. After a couple of months the building looks transformed. The old guard is impressed. Only then do they receive a letter increasing the tariff. But, in deference to their seniority, they don't have to pay full-bore. I usually give them a $10 or $15 a month discount from the rate new tenants are paying. If I had come in and charged them this rate initially, they would have felt as though they were being had. Now, with the improvements and a chance to acclimate themselves to what new tenants are paying, they think they are getting a bargain. I rarely lose tenants from rent increases.

Another common tendency among owners is to become complacent after they have raised rents. This manifests itself in two ways: they may become slipshod with the service they give tenants once they have accomplished their rent goals, or they may miss future opportunities to further increase rents. Both are errors. Excellent ongoing service is a must. Word of mouth is the top source of new tenants, and a happy tenant is the best advertisement.

Tenants are not onerous low-lifers; they are my clients. Rather than ducking their problems, I confront them. Listening to their needs results in a lucrative source of revenue. Besides keeping a tenant happy, it allows me to raise rents. I view their needs as opportunities. If a tenant is displeased with perfectly good wallpaper, rather than tell her, "There's nothing wrong with it; you'll just have to live with it," I gladly change it. I explain, however, that this is expensive and, although I will be happy to advance the costs, I will have to raise the rent $5 per month. The manager and the tenant then work together selecting an appropriate pattern. The same is true for paneling, drapes, painting, carpeting, whatever they want. I just figure my cost, then jack up the rent accordingly. To calculate how much to raise the rent, I estimate the usable life of the improvement, then raise the rent sufficiently to recoup my costs by the time one-third of the usable life-span has expired. For example, let's say there is perfectly good green carpeting in a unit, but the tenant can't stand it. She wants it taken out and replaced with gold carpeting that goes with her furniture. The cost of replacing the carpeting is $500. It has a usable life of five years. One-third of five years is one and two-third years, or twenty months. And $500 divided by twenty months is $25 per month. I tell the tenant we can replace the existing carpeting if she is willing to pay an additional $25 per month. You'll be amazed how often they accept. The manager makes sure the tenant is pleased with the choice. The old carpeting is carefully removed, and stored for future use. Who knows? The next tenant may hate gold carpeting and crave a lovely green. For a small monthly increase, we can probably give her just what she wants.

By satisfying tenant requests, I am constantly raising rents while improving the property. Rents go up, the value of the building increases, and the tenants are pleased. The best of all possible worlds.

Investing in real estate is fun for me. The more I do it, the greater my insights. Of all the available investment modalities, real estate, year in and year out, is consistently the most profitable.

IV

How to Establish and Use Credit

● The old saying, "It takes money to make money" is true! And the more of someone else's money you have at your disposal, the greater your chances of success. Yet many people feel extremely insecure with borrowed funds. For some, they have an almost immoral cast. I recently had a discussion on this subject with a well-to-do Beverly Hills housewife. She and her husband have a net worth of about $500,000. He had just taken out a $25,000 loan for a particularly attractive real-estate partnership. The deal had a guaranteed 10-percent return, plus 50 percent of the profits upon sale. The bank had given him a one-year note at 8 percent. At worst he would make 2 percent on the bank's money with a chance of making a bundle. But his fashionable wife was fretting as though he had committed their last sou: "We've never had to borrow money before. What if something happens? I don't care how much we can make; it's how much we can lose that matters. I told him that if we don't have the money, we shouldn't have gone into the deal."

A few minutes later the subject of dividends and interest was raised. Again the stylish woman spoke up: "I can't tell you what a thrill it was for me to go to the savings and loan the other day and see that *my* account had accrued $256 in interest. It was the greatest feeling in the world. Like finding money!"

This attitude is common. Borrowing money is risky business. Depositing money is security. To be fair, this argument is meaningful for someone who hasn't the foggiest idea of what to do with the borrowed funds. I wouldn't recommend a savings and loan as a home for money, but might not find much fault with high-grade corporate bonds for a financial neophyte. For those with some financial ingenuity, however, the phobia about using borrowed money is misplaced. Borrowed funds are a one-way ticket to financial security, allowing the user to leapfrog several plateaus in his quest. In the above example, this lady's husband had an ironclad deal. Certainly he was correct in borrowing the funds. If fault existed, it was that he didn't borrow more. Deals like that don't pop up every day.

There are basically five ways to obtain wealth. First, be born to it. Second, work your way into a high-paying job and grind it out in spite of bad investment judgment. Third, start with a solid base, as in the second way, and use accumulated funds and borrowing power wisely to reach financial goals early. Fourth, start with little, but finesse your way into the mainstream of borrowed funds and use these as a basis for the accumulation of wealth. Fifth, steal.

Let's eliminate the first and last of these methods

as impractical, and concentrate on the more obtainable solutions.

Working hard all our lives and having it pay off in the long run is what we are conditioned to from childhood. A good education, followed by patient step-by-step advances, eventually brings in the money. High-income earners work the first six months of the year for the government, and the last six months for themselves. Free-spending habits and speculative investments keep many of them lean for years, but they finally get their nest egg prior to retirement.

Some people with prestigious jobs use their power and influence to establish credit. This, combined with their earning power, gives them access to funds when investment opportunities arise. If investments go bad, they use their earning power to bail themselves out. If they are clever, they cut short the road to success. The way they look at the cost of money is simple — since they are in the 50-percent bracket the government pays half the interest. An 8-percent loan really costs them only 4 percent. At this low cost for money, it's difficult for a resourceful man to refuse.

Some don't have the luxury of a power base and a fat salary to commandeer credit lines. They get by on charm, interpersonal competence, and careful planning. Their own resources and earning power provide no visibility for financial independence, so they look elsewhere for money and figure out how to tap it.

Suppose you are a few years out of college and are earning $15,000 a year working for an insurance company. Your wife teaches school and nets another

$8,000 annually. Your yearly family income is $23,000, enough for you to live comfortably, but not enough to accumulate any real money. It looks like the start of one of those thirty-five-year careers of scratching and clawing that will finally eke out enough to allow you to retire at age sixty-five with the help of the corporate pension plan and Social Security. Not a bad posture; many adopt it. But suppose you are the type that would like to bypass a few steps in this grueling process. You are bright and personable, and you realize there is easier money to be made. All you need is a source of capital.

With this goal in mind, you introduce yourself to the vice-president at the local bank that houses your checking account. You've banked there for the past couple of years, although your accounts have never exactly had standout balances. The checking account has had an average balance of $500, and you have $2,000 in savings. You make a point of periodically making contact with the vice-president on subsequent visits to the bank. Then, one day, when the banks are flush with money (you'll be able to tell by the amount of billboard and radio advertising for loans), you call the vice-president for an appointment. Tell him you've banked at *his* branch for several years and that you have been impressed with how efficiently the branch is run. Then say that you and your wife have not taken a vacation in two years and that you don't want to dip into your savings. (Bankers like this; they think you are prudent not to touch your nest egg.) You'd like to borrow $2,000 for a vacation loan.

The banker looks at your "record" and sees little

exposure. Steady job, good banking record, savings account. Looks good. He offers you his standard "installment" loan, but you tell him you prefer a straight six-month note. Yes, you feel comfortable paying it off in six months, no problem. You agree on an interest rate (probably a little higher than you would like); he runs a credit check, asks you to fill out a financial statement, and hands over a cashier's check for the $2,000.

Instead of hopping the first plane to the Caribbean, however, you take the $2,000 down the street to another bank. You walk in and ask to see its vice-president. Tell him you have heard excellent reports about their service. You need a bank you can rely on. No, you have no immediate needs, but want to open a checking account with $2,000. Run a few pay checks through this account to show some activity, but always maintain a balance of at least $2,000. Sixty days later, make an appointment with the same vice-president. Ask him to lunch. Over a martini tell him you need $4,000; you'd like to take a vacation and need the balance to fix up your house. He checks your balances, sees that fat $2,000+ average balance, and gladly makes the loan, provided that you leave a minimum of $1,000 in your checking account at all times as a "compensating balance." Agreed.

You take the $4,000 to a third bank and ask to meet a senior bank officer, casually waving the cashier's check in front of the receptionist. Meet the man, deposit the $4,000, and repeat the process. Borrow $8,000 and use $6,000 to pay off the other banks. Deposit the excess funds in the checking account of your original bank. A couple of months later, go back to this first bank and borrow more money — say, $8,000. Use this to pay the $8,000 you owe bank number three.

What results from all these shenanigans? Simply this — you have established yourself as a credit-worthy customer at three banks. You borrowed money and paid it back *before* it was due. In addition, you maintained sizable balances in checking and savings accounts, balances that the bank used to make money. You have become a "preferred" client. It has cost you about $500 to do this, but you can now borrow $15,000 to $20,000! You can probably stretch your six-month terms to a year and be able to renew for another six months if you wish.

The key words in the money-lending business are "establish a track record." When you borrow and repay, you are establishing such a track record. When you pay *before* a note is due, you go to the front of the class. Once you have borrowed and repaid a few loans, there are no more credit checks, no more "loan committees," no more red tape. You state your needs and your banker fills them. He reaches in his drawer and pulls out a note. You're home free. He may occasionally ask you for an updated financial statement for his files, but this will, of course, look better and better as you put your new-found funds to use. Once you have working capital, the rest is up to you.

If you invest wisely, your financial position will soar. As your net worth increases, so does your borrowing power. The more you borrow and repay, the more the bank wants to give you. It may be hard to believe, but within a few years your borrowing power is likely to be in six figures! And on just a signature. No collateral. Believe me — I've done it! But how can banks lend you hundreds of thousands when you are still only making $23,000 a year? Track record. You pay your debts. You've proven it. And you have shown them that you use their money wisely. Witness your blossoming financial statement. You can reach a financial goal of say $1,000,000 and *never* make more than $23,000 a year in salary.

For some, this running around from bank to bank may be frightening. Understandable. The same objectives can be accomplished, if you're willing to be more patient, with a single bank. A friend of mine, with an annual salary of under $20,000, started eleven years ago with a $1,500 loan from his bank. He has stayed with this same bank ever since, watched six different branch managers come and go, and has borrowed and repaid over $600,000! His current credit line is $75,000. And his interest cost is 1 percent over prime.

This individual *retired* three years ago and currently lives on his investment income. His net worth is currently $1,200,000. He did it *all* on the bank's money. He *never* made more than $20,000 in salary. Most of his money was made in income property, with a few well-timed stock-market investments sprinkled in. And he did it all using only one tiny branch office of a major bank. He didn't have a high-paying, prestigious job, but he had even a stronger influence going for him — a track record. In eleven years and $600,000 of borrowings he was never late in repaying a loan. In fact, he was usually early.

During a period when money was particularly tight, he had $50,000 out on a signature. A senior loan officer, in a review of outstanding debts, came across my friend's loan. Despite his track record and rave reviews from the officers at his branch, the examiner thought the loan was weak, based on fundamentals. He wanted the loan called immediately.

The branch officer, after long argument, convinced the examiner to agree to reducing the outstanding balance to $25,000 instead of calling for the whole thing. My wayward friend was in Europe at the time, but made a transatlantic call in response to the bank's urgent messages. The branch officer, embarrassed by what he felt was a compromised position (his judgment had been questioned), hemmed and hawed on the phone, but finally spat out the bad news. In three days a cashier's check arrived at the branch, not for $25,000, but for the full $50,000.

A few months later, when credit conditions eased, the bank came crawling back to my friend, looking for worthy outlets for the glut of money accumulating in its vaults. My friend demanded a sit-down with the branch officer *and* the senior loan officer who had questioned the wisdom of the previous loan. He went in armed with financial statements showing dramatic yearly increases in his net worth and with detailed, exemplary payment records. He pointed out that he had paid over $40,000 in interest over the years. He also tactfully indicated that he had paid off a surprise call, and had paid off *twice* what they had requested within three days. Using "I" language, he let the senior loan officer know how embarrassed and hurt he felt at what seemed to be a lack of confidence in him. The outcome of the meeting was the establishment of his current $75,000 unsecured line of credit at 1 percent over prime, and the cementing of a tight relationship with the senior loan officer, who was completely won over.

The branch officer, on the recommendation of the senior loan officer, was promoted to district supervisor a few months later. He now supervises the new branch officer, who is carefully instructed to meet my friend's every need. His track record and perceptive handling of unforeseen situations have catapulted this client to the forefront of this bank's VIP list.

ESTABLISHING A PERSONAL RELATIONSHIP WITH YOUR BANKER

By now it must be clear that it is imperative to establish personal relationships with *everyone* important to your success. Your banker is no exception. Again, reversing the "normal" business role is effective. Asking him to lunch, instead of waiting for an invite, changes the role relationship and paves the way for successful negotiation. Cultivating close contact is advisable, including tennis, golf, dinners, hunting trips, or whatever else you may be able to offer to curry his good graces.

When I have a money-making investment, the first person I call, after committing myself and my clients, is my banker. Then, my broker. I try not to overlook opportunities that will make money for people I need, especially if it costs me nothing. I always get *quid pro quo,* usually without asking. A synergistic, close-working relationship is established. Filling his intangible needs is also important, and must not be overlooked.

WHY IT'S GOOD TO OWE MONEY

Contrary to the popular cry voiced earlier in this chapter regarding insecurity feelings associated with borrowed funds, I would feel far more insecure if I didn't owe money. Let's look at the facts:

1) The dollar is steadily depreciating. Money borrowed now is repaid with dollars having far less buying power.

2) Interest on loans is a deductible expense. The government shares in the cost of your loan.

3) A source of investment funds provides the flexibility needed to take advantage of business opportunities that require fast action. Good deals are not available indefinitely, and having the capability to act is a major asset.

4) Bank funds can be used as "seed money" in highly leveraged deals. Maybe all you need to close a lucrative $250,000 real-estate deal is $20,000. The profits from this deal, besides casting a more favorable light on your financial statement, can be pyramided into the next, larger real-estate deal.

Having a source of money unfetters financial creativity. It totally changes investment perspective. Used wisely, it dramatically simplifies making money.

BORROWING FROM FRIENDS

Friendship and money are a treacherous combination. They just don't seem to mix. Investing with friends is fine, but loaning or borrowing money is fraught with problems.

This quote from *Hamlet* sums it up:

> Neither a borrower nor a lender be;
> For loan oft loses both itself and friend,
> And borrowing dulls the edge of husbandry.
> — SHAKESPEARE

I follow this rule with friends: *Never borrow, never lend.* I stick to it faithfully. Years ago, the few experiences I had lending money met with total loss — I lost the money *and* the friend. Pass.

CASH FLOW

Cash flow is the net of money in and money out. Suppose you have $3,000 coming in and $3,000 going out. When all transactions settle, you will be even. But if the $3,000 comes in thirty days before you have to pay, you will have the use of $3,000 for thirty days. This is the equivalent of a thirty-day interest-free loan. If you can do this consistently over the years, the use of interest-free money can result in the accumulation of a small fortune.

Credit cards are an excellent source of positive cash flow. If you pay the entire monthly balance due before the next statement is issued, there are no interest or finance charges. It takes about thirty to sixty days from the time you sign for a credit voucher to appear on your monthly statement. Then you have an *additional* thirty days to pay before charges accrue. The net effect is sixty to ninety days of interest-free money!

I request maximum credit limits, usually $3,000 to $5,000 per card. I have every major card. Some of the cards have "ready reserve accounts." This means that if my checking account is overdrawn at the bank issuing the card, the overdraft is automatically covered and charged to my credit card. Wonderful! Free money! A reserve for those occasions when I'm scratching for cash to close a deal. Sometimes this extra little bit makes a difference. I pay whenever possible with a credit card. Air fares, dining out, clothing purchases, gasoline, massages, theater tickets, bicycles, golf clubs — you name it. I get sixty- to ninety-day terms, at no interest. My money works for me until the last moment; then the outstanding balance is paid. By using this "float," I make over $1,000 a year! As a spin-off, my credit rating is superb. No matter how high my credit balances, I *always* pay in full before the next statement. This makes me A1. The credit-card companies keep increasing my limit.

When a credit check is being made, I list all my cards as reference. They give me their highest rating. Actually, it's costing them plenty to have me as a customer. Besides the cost of handling, mailing, processing, et cetera, they are letting me use their money, without charge, for sixty to ninety days. If everyone did this, the credit-card companies would go bankrupt in short order.

Cash flow can also be maximized in other areas. Bill paying, for example. The telephone and electric company won't hassle you if you pay in forty-five to sixty days; attorneys, accountants, doctors, and dentists ninety to one hundred and twenty days. Hotels and restaurants (once you have established credit) also ninety to one hundred and twenty days. I've even gone so far as to run a tab at a local restaurant for one hundred and twenty days, then pay by *credit card,* deferring *my* payment for an additional sixty days. I'm being carried for six months! No problems. Still a preferred customer at the restaurant (they *always* get paid) and at the credit-card companies.

The point is this: We live in a credit world. Businesses are accustomed to extending credit when they feel assured of being paid. It's a cost of doing business. It's only right that their better clients avail themselves of this service. Contrary to what you may think, stretching out payment does not mar my credit rating. I have regular, personal contact with many of my creditors and they feel quite comfortable with the arrangement. If anyone were to call them for a reference, they would give me a glowing report. Remember, they always get paid *in full.* I avoid partial payments. They are a sign of weakness. I *never* make partial payments. Better to pay in full thirty days later than to pay part. Each month I review all my outstanding bills, making careful assessments. I know which bills to pay and which to defer. Try it. A little practice and suddenly you'll have money left over at the end of the month.

V

The Subtleties of Swiss Banking

STABILITY

● It has become very *en vogue* to have a Swiss bank account. It is estimated that perhaps 100,000 Americans currently have accounts in Switzerland. What is the fascination of this natural-resource impoverished, tiny country (about two-thirds the size of West Virginia)? In a word — stability. Look at the facts:

1) Switzerland remained neutral in World War I and World War II, despite being surrounded by Germany, France, Italy, and Austria.
2) The current unemployment rate is 0.5 percent. Only 14,000 people in the entire country are out of work.
3) The inflation rate is about 1 percent.
4) Due to the shortage of natural resources the Swiss market their services, and banking is the biggest service industry in Switzerland.

5) The country sports some 500 banks; one for every 10,000 people.
6) Being so financially oriented, the Swiss have acquired a reputation for making sound investments. Many accounts are managed on a discretionary basis.
7) The Swiss franc has seven times the gold backing of the American dollar.
8) The Swiss believe that an individual's financial dealings are private. It is a *criminal offense* for any bank employee to divulge information about any client.
9) Governmental authority is limited. Personal liberty is stressed.

Small wonder there has been a steady stream of money flowing through, over, and around the mountains that surround Switzerland.

SWISS-BANK SECRECY

Throughout the years, despite tremendous pressures, the Swiss have maintained their financial integrity and the anonymity of their clients. They play no favorites! In the late 1930s billions of dollars flowed out of Germany into Switzerland as tens of thousands of Jews tried to protect their funds from confiscation by the Third Reich. Despite the renowned efficiency and pressures of Nazi and Gestapo agents, the Swiss tenaciously refused to reveal the identities of their depositors.

During World War II, the Swiss banks sent their gold reserves to New York branches for safekeeping.

The United States Government, suspecting that a large portion of these holdings were from German depositors, demanded to know the identity of the account holders. The New York branches of the Swiss banks told United States Government investigators that all deposits were in the name of Swiss banks. The United States turned the screws. They demanded the *true* identity of the account holders and froze the gold reserves. From the summer of 1941 to 1946 the Americans kept Swiss assets locked up tightly in New York, while negotiations with the Swiss continued. For additional leverage, the government threatened to cut off Swiss supplies. The countries surrounding the Swiss borders were completely controlled by the Allies, so the threat had teeth. Finally, after five long years of holding out, the Swiss reluctantly agreed to a compromise. They would seize German assets held in Switzerland and divide the proceeds of the seizure with the Allies. In exchange, the United States would release the frozen funds and renew normal relations with Switzerland.

Did this agreement jeopardize the financial stability that had withstood two wars and a whole slew of investigators from indignant governments? Not in the least! In classic style, the Swiss methodically proceeded to make sure that every German depositor got back *all* the funds American pressures had forced them to confiscate. The result was a strengthening of the world outlook on Swiss-bank security measures and a renewed respect for the integrity of the Swiss. The Swiss banks' reputation escaped unscathed! They had protected the identity of their Nazi depositors with the same tenacity and zeal they had used to protect Jewish funds a few years before. Absolute nondiscrimination! Equal protection for all under the banking code!

Pressures on the Swiss banking system have been constant. Whenever economic uncertainty abounds anywhere in the world, funds inevitably migrate into the dependable Swiss vaults, and a new government tries its hand at cracking Swiss secrecy measures. Extortion, threats, bribes — you name it — they've been unsuccessfully tried on the resolute Swiss. The Germans, British, and Italians all failed.

Recent pressures from the United States are viewed by the Swiss as the most dangerous. In private, Swiss bankers are convinced that the ultimate test of Swiss-bank secrecy will come from confrontations with Washington. The independent Swiss have become closely aligned with the States both financially and in matters of trade. And United States officials have continued to exert constant pressure in their attempts to pierce the secrecy veil. They have opened up a tiny fissure in the granite Swiss front — the banking treaty of 1975. This agreement provides for the release of banking information to United States authorities if there is conclusive proof, to the satisfaction of the banking commission in Bern, that a criminal act has been committed, and that funds related to this act are being held in Switzerland. Tax evasion is *not* a crime in Switzerland. It is considered a private matter between an individual and his government. The Swiss will not recognize IRS inquiries per se. Evidence of a felonious offense by *Swiss standards* is required for the release of information.

Nevertheless, knowledgeable Swiss bankers are concerned that the United States has its big foot in the door. Although memories of the 1940s have dimmed, they have not been forgotten, and Swiss bankers fear the power and persistence of the United States.

A big scandal, in the spring of 1977, created a new threat to Swiss bank secrecy. This menace came from a most unlikely source — the Swiss themselves. The Chiasso branch of one of the "big three" Swiss banks, the Swiss Credit Bank (Credit Suisse), guaranteed a number of loans for Texon Finanzanstalt, a Liechtenstein Anstalt (corporation). These guarantees went to a group of about one thousand Italians and a few banks, and totaled an unbelievable $870,000,000. As surprising as the size of the guarantees are, it's even more puzzling that they weren't entered on the bank's books! The guarantees were unauthorized! Credit Swiss headquarters in Zurich knew nothing about them. When Texon Finanzanstalt came up lame, the result was mayhem! Swiss Credit Corp's stock plunged 35 percent in a week. A raft of arrests and suicides followed, and the whole issue of banking controls and secrecy was reopened. The Swiss are still trying to pick up the pieces. This was, undoubtedly, a dark day for Swiss banking. It is a black spot on the previously unblemished Swiss integrity. The result will be a crackdown on *internal controls*. Bern will take steps to see that such mishaps don't occur in the future. But for the rest of us it will be business as usual. This will not be the beginning of the end for bank secrecy. The Swiss will overcome it. And it will take a lot more pressure than the United States has exerted to date to crack the ledgers of Swiss-account holders.

The truth is that, if Swiss bank secrecy were no more, it would result in a mass exodus of funds. For years other countries have unsuccessfully tried to compete with the Swiss for funds and, if secrecy breaks down, it will open up the underbellies of the Swiss banks to foreign assault. The tiny principality of Liechtenstein, for one, would be waiting with lapping tongue should the mighty weaken (see next chapter, page 194). So the Swiss have a lot at stake in their battle to preserve privacy. As sagacious and persevering as they have been over the decades, they are not likely to endanger their largest industry — the consequences would be grave indeed!

INSIDE A SWISS BANK

There are several types of Swiss banks. The kind that capture my fancy are the private banks. These, as the name implies, are owned by private individuals and families, and they typify the Swiss at their banking best. My first trip to one of these hideaways was very exciting. I felt the same tingling in my groin that I felt when I first landed in New York City. My excitement soon waned, however, when I couldn't find the place. Wandering in a seemingly endless labyrinth of narrow streets, I made frequent inquiries as to the bank's whereabouts. Although most people eagerly offered me an opinion as to the bank's location, no two opinions were the same. It was like the blind leading the blind!

Finally I stumbled on a blank façade I had passed half a dozen times. I searched the nooks and crannies of the building's exterior like Sherlock Holmes looking for a secret entrance. And there it was! In tarnished, six-inch-high brass letters, the bank's name. As I stepped on the threshold, a door magically slid open and I was in. Instantly I was greeted by three uniformed guards (they all spoke English) and escorted into a small, soundproof cubicle, richly done up in wood, leather, and plush carpeting. I gave one of the guards the name of the banker I wanted to see. A few minutes later the guard reappeared and asked me to follow him. Onto a small elevator we went (both of us) and emerged three floors up (more guards). I was escorted to a larger version of the downstairs cubicle, with a neatly laid-out table and four chairs in its center. My escort disappeared.

A few minutes later a man wearing a business suit entered — obviously not a guard. He introduced himself (indeed, this was the banker) and asked if he could get me a drink.

"Coffee?" I asked.

"Of course," he said. "Black?"

"Yes," I answered, half-dazed by the fanfare.

He reached for the telephone. Within moments a uniformed butler (different uniform than the guards) arrived with a serving tray. Expresso in a porcelain cup, lemon peel, and bit of marzipan. The banker drank Perrier water with a wedge of lime. There was a certain discernible difference between this and the twenty-year-old blond teller at Bank of America! No neon signs, no logos, no billboards — just uniformed guards and butlers and tasteful little counting rooms where I could imagine generations of kings and countesses counting out suitcases full of money.

I told the banker I represented certain large clients, and gave him the name of the person who had referred me. Without revealing even a glimmer of recognition, he asked how he could be of service. Surprisingly, the meeting lasted three hours! He called in experts in different areas of foreign currency trading, stocks, bonds, gold, et cetera. The bank even had its own in-house legal counsel, and my host marched him up to help resolve some technical issues. All in all, it was a bravado performance. When the parade finally ended, I felt as if I had been thoroughly indoctrinated in many of the available possibilities of Swiss banking.

As I look back on it now, that was merely an hors d'oeuvre. These aren't banks at all, at least not as we know them. They are a conglomeration of money managers, stock brokers, currency experts, real-estate agents, estate planners, corporate lawyers, international tax consultants, confidants, and connoisseurs. Formidable! Unlike the anal retentive types that hold down chairs in many banks in this country, these folks are creative. All they ask is that you clearly state your needs. Then, if they can't fill them, they know someone who can. Instead of trying to tell you *why you can't* do something, they marshal their prodigious ingenuity and considerable resources toward figuring out *how you can*. A refreshing approach.

MORAL AND LEGAL ISSUES

"What is moral is what you feel good after and what is immoral is what you feel bad after."
— ERNEST HEMINGWAY

Before we get caught up in the intricacies of Swiss banking, let's first examine some basic issues. I want to clearly distinguish legal issues from moral issues. As a United States citizen you are *legally* required to:

1) Report any foreign bank accounts on your Federal-income-tax statement.
2) Report cash, cash equivalents, or negotiable securities in excess of $5,000 when either leaving or entering the United States.
3) Report funds in excess of $5,000 being sent out of the country.
4) Report any bank accounts for any foreign corporation, establishment, trust, or fiduciary in which you are the majority shareholder.
5) Pay taxes on all income derived from foreign investments.

As far as *moral* issues are concerned, it's up to each individual to search his conscience to ascertain what course provides the least discomfort. You may feel that it is a frank invasion of your privacy to have to report to the government what you do with your money. What business is it of theirs, as long as you pay your taxes? On the other hand, you may feel that Uncle has a right to know what you do with your funds, and needs this information to *protect* your inalienable rights as a United States citizen. What you do must come from within. Salve your own conscience.

The future looks like this:

1) The United States, like many other countries, will get progressively more restrictive about currency flows out of the country. Laws will be passed to choke off the outflow of capital.
2) It may become illegal to have a foreign bank account.
3) Penalties for failure to comply with existing statutes are likely to become more severe.

The reason for this is fear. The dollar has not exactly been a sterling performer in recent years relative to the strong currencies of the world. In fact, it's been the pits! Big government, big spending, and big budget and trade deficits have knocked the wind out of the dollar. Citizens, legitimately trying to protect their earnings, have become progressively restless at the constant erosion of their currency and, quite naturally, have looked elsewhere for solace. This efflux of capital has resulted in some restrictions and there are more to come. Instead of looking homeward to try to correct the self-induced excesses, our leaders have tried to make it tough for those seeking self-protection. And so the ball gets thrown right back in your lap. What to do? The choice is yours. You must decide what, or who, comes first.

FOREIGN CURRENCIES

United States banks do not provide an active foreign-currency market. Swiss banks do. You don't have to be a maven to figure out that it is wise to diversify your assets into several different currencies. Most of us wouldn't dream of sinking everything into one stock, no matter how much we liked it, so why do so on a single currency? I'm convinced that if foreign-currency trading were easy in America, a vast majority of investors would diversify. Since it's not readily available, relatively few people have gone to the trouble. But it's costly to be lazy. Over the past five years the Swiss franc and German mark have appreciated about 50 percent against the dollar. If you had done *nothing* but buy francs and marks five years ago, you would have a 50-percent profit — by buying money! Liquid! Easily convertible! Spends well! "Ah, but this is hindsight," you say. If you had bought pounds, lira, or French francs, you would have gotten dinged. And if you had taken a flier with pesos or cruzeiros, you would have successfully turned hard currency into Charmin.

I follow two simple rules in currency diversifisation:

1) The strong get stronger; the weak get weaker.
2) Political and social unrest leads to currency weaknesses.

If you follow these two principles, you will do well. At the time of this writing, the strong currencies are the Swiss franc, German mark, and Japanese yen. The weak currencies are the lira, peso, cruzeiro, pound, French franc, Canadian dollar, and U.S. dollar. No real surprises. The only change in the last three years has been a strengthening of the yen to strong currency status and a weakening of the Canadian dollar from strong to weak.

The demise of the Canadian dollar illustrates point two. In 1975 and 1976 the Canadian dollar was a strong performer. I used Canadian dollars along with Swiss francs and German marks in several portfolios I manage. In November, 1976, elections were being held in Quebec. From some of my Canadian contacts I got wind that the Parti Québecois was gaining momentum and had a good chance of winning the election. On election eve the Canadian dollar was worth about $1.02 U.S. The Parti Québecois is a separatist party — they want to separate Quebec from the rest of Canada. Since Montreal is the seat of a great number of corporate headquarters for Canadian companies, the idea of separation left the financial community rather cold. To put this in perspective, it is like an American political party whose platform advocates secession of New York from the United States. Kind of catchy, but likely to cause the rest of the world to wonder what kind of mushrooms they've been eating. At any rate, the race in Quebec looked close enough to warrant a trip, so I zipped up to Montreal and settled in front of a TV set to watch the election returns. By midnight it was clear that the separatists had won.

There is a five-hour time difference between

Montreal and the Continent, so I requested a 3 A.M. wake-up, (8 A.M. European time), and placed some orders for my accounts. My instructions were to convert all Canadian-dollar positions to Swiss francs and to *short* Canadian dollars on 90-percent margin! My reasoning was this: There was no way this victory could be construed as being good for Canada. A can of worms had been opened and the rest of the world was likely to look on these developments with a jaundiced eye. I saw virtually no near-term upside potential and substantial downside risk for the Canadian currency. The rest is history. I covered our short positions a few weeks later at 96 cents U.S. — a 65-percent profit on our leveraged short position! The Canadian dollar has continued to erode slowly. In March, 1978, it was worth about 89 cents U.S. So long as the Quebec situation is unresolved, there will be a cloud over this currency.

Another example of a currency likely to plummet is the Spanish peseta. When the long reign of Franco ended, the leadership of Spain went up for grabs. Political groups are still jockeying for position, with the Socialists in the lead. Recently the Communists gained a foothold, a party totally suppressed under Franco. At present, political uncertainty abounds in Spain and this spells trouble for the peseta. I look for it to be under pressure.

France is another political hot spot, a country in which there are numerous political factions. No one faction is strong enough to control the government. The existing ruling coalition is doomed. The Gaulists, under the leadership of the mayor of Paris, Jacques Chirac, are becoming progressively more powerful, but not quite strong enough to control a majority of the vote. Meantime, the labor unions are out of control. At a whim they paralyze the city, stopping the Metro, turning off the traffic lights, and refusing to collect garbage. They are a powerful, headstrong group. The only thing that's clear about the French scene is that the government is in a state of turmoil. According to rule two, this makes the French franc a no-no. Indeed, it has depreciated about 25 percent over the past two years against the strong currencies.

SECURITIES

Stocks — Swiss banks trade securities in all major markets: New York, London, Zurich, Paris, Frankfurt, Tokyo, Milan. All securities are purchased in the name of the Swiss bank, insuring privacy. At present I find the United States, Zurich, and Frankfurt markets most intriguing. The United States stock market is far and away the world's leader. The wealth of United States industry is staggering, and the United States securities markets tend to set the trend for the rest of the world. The United States economy strongly influences the economies of Western Europe and Japan. It led them into the 1974–1975 recession and has set the pace for the current world economic recovery. Foreign stock markets parallel price changes in New York. Within a few days of a Wall Street rally, the rising tide ripples through the European stock exchanges. Indeed, some very sharp European traders closely monitor the New York markets and successfully trade stocks in Europe. Using United States markets as a yardstick, they tell me that European market moves are predictable 90 percent of the time!

The Zurich and Frankfurt markets hold my interest for two important reasons — Swiss francs and German marks. All trades in Zurich are conducted in francs and all trades in Frankfurt are in marks. This is an ideal method of capitalizing on the strength of the strong foreign currencies, while participating in American industry and receiving dividends. That's right! I said *American* industry, for a number of American companies have their shares listed on foreign exchanges. Tables 1 and 2 (on pp. 172–74) list American companies on the Zurich and Frankfurt exchanges, respectively. You can buy shares in American companies in francs or marks, receive dividends in these strong currencies, and combine the stock-market theories of Chapter II (p. 58) with strong currency diversification. And all in absolute privacy.

I limit investments on foreign exchanges to United States companies whose fundamentals I know and understand. It's just too much work to try to stay on top of corporations in other countries. If you are interested, however, your Swiss bank probably houses an expert in the major European exchanges and will gladly arrange an audience for you.

Besides the currency play, there is another advantage to buying United States stocks on foreign exchanges — commissions. The commissions on the Zurich stock exchange are standardized — 1 percent in; 1 percent out. Compare these with the rates you are currently paying. Unless you are dealing with a discount

TABLE 1

AMERICAN STOCKS LISTED
ON THE ZURICH STOCK EXCHANGE

Aetna Life and Casualty
Company
Amax Inc.
American Cyanamid
Company
American Telephone &
Telegraph Co.
Beatrice Foods Co.
The Black and Decker
Manufacturing Co.
Borden, Inc.
Burlington Industries, Inc.
Burroughs Corporation
Caterpillar Tractor Co.
Chessie System, Inc.
Chrysler Corporation
City Investing Company
The Coca-Cola Company
Colgate Palmolive
Company
Consolidated Natural Gas
Co.
Continental Group, Inc.
Continental Oil Company
Control Data Corporation
Corning Glass Works
CPC International Inc.
Crown Zellerbach
Corporation
Dow Chemical Company
E. I. du Pont de Nemours &
Co.

Eastman Kodak Company
Exxon Corporation
The Firestone Tire &
Rubber Co.
Ford Motor Company
General Electric Co.
General Foods Corporation
General Motors Corporation
General Telephone &
Electronics Corp.
The Gillette Company
Goodyear Tire & Rubber
Co.
W. R. Grace & Co.
Gulf & Western Industries,
Inc.
Halliburton Company
Honeywell Inc.
Inco Limited
International Business
Machines Corp.
International Paper
Company
International Telephone
and Telegraph Corp.
Kennecott Copper Corp.
Kraft, Inc.
Lily (Eli) and Company
Litton Industries Inc.
Minnesota Mining &
Manufacturing Co.
Mobil Corporation

Monsanto Company
National Distillers and
    Chemical Corp.
NCR Corporation
Norton Simon
Owens-Illinois, Inc.
Pacific Gas & Electric Co.
Penn Central Company
PepsiCo, Inc.
Phillip Morris Inc.
Phillips Petroleum
    Company
The Procter & Gamble
    Company
Rockwell International
    Corporation
Smith Kline Corporation
Sperry Rand Corporation

Squibb Corporation
Standard Oil Company
    (Indiana)
Texaco Inc.
Transamerica Corporation
Union Carbide Corp.
Uniroyal Inc.
United States Gypsum
    Company
United States Steel
    Corporation
United Technologies
    Corporation
Warner-Lambert Company
F.W. Woolworth Co.
Xerox Corporation
Zenith Radio Corporation

TABLE 2

AMERICAN STOCKS LISTED
ON THE FRANKFURT STOCK EXCHANGE

Caterpillar
CBS Inc.
Chase Manhattan Corp.
Chrysler Corp.
Coca-Cola Company
Colgate Palmolive
    Company
Continental Group, Inc.
Continental Oil Company
Control Data Corp.
Deere & Company
Diamond Shamrock Corp.
Dow Chemical Company

E. I. Du Pont de Nemours
    & Co.
Exxon Corp.
Firestone Tire & Rubber
    Company
Ford Motor Company
General Motors Corp.
Goodyear Tire & Rubber
W. R. Grace & Company
International Business
    Machines Corp.
International Telephone
    and Telegraph Corp.

TABLE 2 (*continued*)

Kraft, Inc.	Procter & Gamble Company
Lehman Corp.	Richardson Merrell Inc.
Litton Industries, Inc.	Sperry Rand Corp.
Minnesota Mining &	Studebaker Worthington
Manufacturing Company	TRW Inc.
Mobil Oil Corp.	United Technologies
Monsanto Company	Corporation
Norton Simon	Warner-Lambert Company
Occidental Petroleum Corp.	Wells Fargo & Company
Phillip Morris Inc.	Xerox Corp.

brokerage house, or have negotiated deep discounts, Zurich rates will save money. In addition, there is no penalty for small orders or odd lots. It's 1 percent for everyone.

Bonds — Not surprisingly, your versatile Swiss bank handles bonds too. The intermediate-sized and larger Swiss banks underwrite new bond issues in Europe. On the Eurobond market the company issuing the bond can choose its currency. Dollar, Swiss franc, and Deutsche mark bonds are the most popular. As in the United States, Eurobonds are rated with yields decreasing as ratings improve. As a rule, yields on Eurobonds are higher than yields on comparably rated companies in the United States. This is an obvious plus. Another advantage is being able to choose the currency you wish. There are plenty of issues in any currency that interests you, so you can take your best shot. What I like is the double protection — yield plus a strong currency play. A concrete example will illustrate these mouthwatering dynamics. In March, 1976, I bought some 8¼-

percent, seven-year, A-rated German mark bonds for some of my accounts. By July, 1977, the following events had transpired:

1) The company had paid 8¼ percent at semiannual intervals (in German marks).
2) The market value of the bonds had appreciated 8 percent ($1080 for each $1000 face amount).
3) The German mark had appreciated 8 percent relative to the U.S. dollar.

What has our conservative bond investment made? Well over 20 percent on an annualized basis. Pretty sweet!

United States companies also issue Eurobonds. These have a higher yield than equivalent issues in the States and may be issued in a number of different currencies, so you need not invest in foreign companies if it makes you nervous. For me, I heed the advice of my Swiss banker. He is current on the financial ratings of foreign borrowers and tends to err on the prudent side when giving counsel.

Convertible Bonds — Eurobonds of non-Swiss companies are exempt from the 35-percent Swiss withholding tax (see Chapter VII).

A convertible bond on the Euromarket combines many of the advantages of stocks and bonds. A convertible is a debt instrument (loan) and as such receives preferred treatment in the event of liquidation of the underlying company. The yield tends to be higher than common-stock dividends and, as the name implies, it can be converted into common stock at a fixed price at any time during its life-span. If the common stock of the company goes up, the owner of the convertible trades in his bonds for shares of common stock at a substantial profit; if the common stock goes down, the convertible is still a binding obligation on the company. When it becomes due and payable, the company must redeem it at *face value* (usually $1,000 units). If you hold a convertible long enough, the *worst* you can do is get your money back plus interest. If at any time during its life-span the stock runs up, you come out swimmingly. In addition, you can buy convertibles in many currencies, including Swiss francs and German marks. Like Euro-bonds, the interest payments on convertibles issued by non-Swiss companies receive preferential tax treatment.

Disadvantages? Minor. For one thing, the yield is not as high as with ordinary bonds. For another, there are fewer convertible issues than straight-debt issues. The lower yield is a minor grievance when compared to the huge plus of convertibility. Although the number of issues is relatively small, if you are patient, you will find high-quality companies issuing European market convertibles in a strong currency at a good time in the stock-market cycle. *Leap* at the opportunity!

TYPES OF SWISS BANK ACCOUNTS

These have been extensively covered in other books on Swiss banks. I'd like to say a word, however, about negative interest on Swiss franc accounts. If you keep your funds in Swiss francs, the bank by law must *charge* you interest on your deposits in excess of $40,000. The charge is 10 percent per quarter! These charges more than counterbalance the likely appreciation of the Swiss franc. The clearly stated purpose of this act is to discourage foreign investors from buying Swiss francs. But, as with most regulations, there is a lacuna for the perceptive investor. You can buy Eurobonds, Euroconverts, or Zurich stock-market holdings in Swiss francs, avoid the negative interest charges, and *collect* interest on your bonds and converts with special tax breaks (see below). Dividends on stocks are taxed at 35 percent, but capital gains are *not* taxed. In short, if you want to hold Swiss francs, don't keep them in the bank. Invest them! This way you will avoid the negative interest, while making sound investments in the world's strongest currency.

For those of you bent on keeping your money in a deposit account, there is another out. The law states that each bank can pay you interest on the first 50,000 Swiss francs ($20,000 U.S.). The next 50,000 Swiss francs receive no interest and no penalty. Anything over 100,000 francs is taxed at the rate of 10 percent per quarter. Accounts in existence prior to October 31, 1974, are exempt from negative interest. But Swiss-bank secrecy protects the identity of account holders from both other banks *and* the Swiss government. So you can open up deposit accounts of 50,000 Swiss francs at as many different banks as you wish and receive interest from each at current rates (3½ percent to 5 percent) without worrying about negative interest charges.

TAXES

Switzerland has *no* capital-gain taxes. The foreign investor can be taxed on income and dividends in a number of ways. It's what I call the 35-percent rule. If your Swiss bank buys United States stocks or bonds, dividend and interest payments are *automatically* taxed by the United States authorities at 35 percent. Your Swiss account will be credited with the remaining 65 percent. If you declare this income on your United States tax returns, you can claim the 35-percent withholding and adjust your taxes either up or down, depending on your bracket. Foreign capital gains are treated by the United States IRS like any other capital gain, and, if declared, will be treated accordingly (short term or long term).

The Swiss authorities tax certain forms of income:

1) Interest earned on savings accounts held at Swiss banks, *regardless* of the currency.
2) Interest paid on Eurocurrencies (Eurodollars, Euromarks, Eurofrancs, et cetera).
3) Interest paid on bonds issued by Swiss companies, regardless of currency.
4) Dividends paid by companies on the Zurich stock exchange.

The notable exception that slips through the fingers of *all* tax authorities are the *bonds and convertible bonds of non-Swiss companies issued in Europe.*

In these cases there is *no* tax on the income, regardless of the currency in which the bond is issued.
Unless you declare the income on your taxes, there will
be no withholdings, deductions, or charges of any kind
(except the small purchase and sale commissions). For
this reason these are the ideal vehicles for yield-ori-
ented investors seeking capital diversification into several currencies.

Other areas that are not taxed by the Swiss and
not reported to anyone are:

1) Profits on gold or silver trading.
2) Profits from real-estate transactions.
3) Profits from currency trading.
4) Profits from trading commodities.
5) Short- or long-term gains from stocks,
   bonds, or convertibles.

PRECIOUS METALS

Although it is now legal for Americans to trade
gold, it is difficult to imagine why anyone would want to
in the United States. First, commissions eat you alive —
a whopping 4 percent round trip. In Zurich it costs a
mere ¾ percent for the same transaction. Second, there
is no privacy when you buy precious metals in the
United States. Every transaction is reported. Next, there
is no United States gold market per se. Prices are
pegged to the London market. Zurich has an *active* gold
market. In short, United States banks and securities
dealers are not yet used to dealing with precious metals
and are not set up for large-scale transactions. For the

Swiss banks these are routine. The banks provide active markets in gold and silver bullion and gold coins of all types. In addition, they can readily participate in the New York or London gold future markets. Your Swiss bank will have a man or a whole department specializing in precious-metal dealings. For my money, I'll stick with the pros, especially when it's cheaper!

HEDGING IN GOLD AND SILVER

I think it is prudent to put 10 percent of your net worth into gold and silver. But, as in any other market, the prices of these metals are influenced by supply-demand forces, and prices can get out of line. In December, 1974, gold skyrocketed to $200 per ounce in anticipation of the legalization of gold ownership by Americans. When this Roman candle fizzled (it appears that those Americans interested in gold *already* owned it), the price plummeted. It bottomed at about $105 per ounce, then started creeping up again. My accounts bought heavily between $110 and $130. In April, 1977, gold was back above $150 per ounce. To me this represented full valuation relative to what I perceived as a pretty-well-controlled worldwide inflation rate for 1977. It didn't seem appropriate to dump our gold holdings, but a little hedging seemed prudent. I accomplished this in two ways:

For some large accounts I *wrote* options against our gold holdings. We were paid $9 per ounce in cash. The buyer received the option to buy our gold at any time between April, 1977, and November, 1977, for

$150 per ounce. The $9 per ounce was ours — gone forever. Gold was selling at $152 per ounce the day the contract was written. We delivered our gold in November for $150 per ounce. When we added the $9 premium, our net was $159 per ounce. If gold had decreased in value, the premium our buyer paid protected us unless gold dropped below $141 per ounce. Our strategy was optimal. Gold stayed in a trading range between $141 and $159.

For a second group of investors I hedged gold profits by using the New York Mercantile Exchange. This parallels the above example. We wrote commodities option contracts for October delivery of gold bullion at $156 per ounce. This *guaranteed* us $156 per ounce for our gold in October, *regardless* of what happened to the price in the interim. In October, had gold been selling at $110 per ounce, we would still have gotten $156 for ours. By the same token, if gold had been selling at $200 per ounce, we would *still* have been obliged to deliver ours for $156. Since we bought back the contracts at $152 in October, we pocketed a small profit and still own our bullion. These types of hedges with gold pay off when gold has run up and is static or drifting off. They lock in your profits and then some!

REAL ESTATE

Your Swiss bank is not a real-estate agency. However, in the typically Swiss resourceful manner, your bank can be a tremendous asset in the purchase and sale of real estate. Here's how:

1) Some banks make real-estate investments for themselves and for selected clients. If you get on the good side of your banker and express an interest in real estate, he may include you in his next syndication.

2) Swiss bankers have tentacles that reach world-wide. They are extremely well connected in international financial circles. It is not uncommon for them to get wind of lucrative real-estate deals. If you play your cards right, you can get them to share their knowledge with you.

3) Your Swiss banker can give you a discreet letter of introduction to select real-estate brokers around the world. Although such letters are not easily obtained, they carry *substantial* impact and can open many doors to juicy real-estate ventures.

4) As your banker learns to know and trust you, he may arrange for you to meet other clients of the bank with shared interests. This can lead to all sorts of possibilities, real estate being near the top of the list.

5) Your Swiss bank can buy real estate for you anywhere in the world in the bank's name, insuring your privacy.

6) Your Swiss bank can arrange for mortgage money, either through foreign banks or Swiss mortgage companies.

7) Swiss bankers can be a valuable source of financial advice. They tend to have their fingers on the international financial pulses and can help you evaluate a prospective investment.

8) The larger Swiss banks have in-house attor-

neys. They can advise you on the legalities of property ownership in various parts of the world, tax consequences, et cetera.

9) There are manifold provocative possibilities for using your Swiss bank creatively in real-estate investments. One Englishman I know bought a combination home and office in the name of his Swiss bank. He then proceeded to *rent* the property from his bank. Of course, all rental payments went straight into his numbered account. In reality, he was writing rent checks to himself. Half the rent went toward his office space, so he deducted this amount from his taxes as a business expense! Writing checks to himself and deducting them as a business expense — a pretty clever way of having the government share in the expenses of his investment!

LIFE INSURANCE

Life insurance is a poor investment and I do *not* recommend it as an investment for anyone. I do, however, recommend term insurance as a means of "insuring" the welfare of your survivors. If your heirs are going to be compensated in the event of your death, they may as well be paid in a hard currency — like Swiss francs, for instance. Once again, call on your friendly Swiss banker. He will refer you to a Swiss life-insurance company where you can get a term life policy with premiums and awards paid in Swiss francs. All payments will be handled per your instructions from your Swiss account.

IN CASE OF DEATH

While we are on the subject of life insurance, I will say a word about estate planning. How are your Swiss accounts passed along in the event of death? When accounts are kept *totally* secret, your money may line the Swiss vaults indefinitely! When you open your account, your banker will have you sign a beneficiary agreement. This agreement names the assignee of your account. It can be changed as often as you like. It is a good idea, however, if *someone* knows who the beneficiary is and at which bank your account resides. I know of several tragic examples in which Swiss account holders died unexpectedly. Their heirs knew there was money in Switzerland, but that's as far as their information went. Without knowing the banks, attempting to locate the accounts was like trying to find the needle in the proverbial haystack, especially when bank secrecy and the close-mouthed Swiss are involved. In one case the family of the deceased have been searching for untold millions for five years now and have come up empty. A trusted attorney or lifelong friend may be a good person to tell. If you present a certified death certificate and proper identification to the right bank assuming ownership is routine. Keep in mind a couple of important principles:

1) A United States will is *not* binding on the Swiss bank. The beneficiary agreement held by the bank is what they will honor.
2) There are no estate taxes due the Swiss

in the event of death. What you do with the United States IRS is up to you. Rest assured that the Swiss bank will not report the proceedings.

THE SWISS BANKERS

Swiss bankers come in all shapes and sizes. They share a few common traits, however. They are a closed-mouthed lot, hardworking and honest. But here the common denominators stop. Some bankers are aloof and to get anything out of them is like pulling teeth. Some bear an open animosity toward American accounts; they just don't seem to want the hassle. Perhaps the memories of World War II American pressures have not been forgotten, or perhaps the constant probes put them off. Some will handle United States accounts only if the account holder waives his secrecy rights. This allows the bank to report openly all transactions. Then there are the other guys. The knowledgeable, helpful, creative financial "wunderkind." They tend to be a tad younger than the former group and much more adventuresome. They seem to thrive on financial dealings. Nothing is impossible. They seek the optimal course of action in problem solving. Decisive, quick, and clever, they will find a way to fill your needs. Although, in typical Swiss style, they tend to warm to you slowly, once drawn out of their shells they are a truly formidable breed!

FILLING THE NEEDS OF YOUR SWISS BANKER

As superhuman as your Swiss banker may appear, he still has needs. Recognition for a job well done goes a long way. Tokens of esteem and friendship are well received. I have found that courtesy and thoughtfulness are returned in kind. Above all, I meet my commitments. If I say I am going to do something, anything, at a certain time, I do it — as planned and on time. The Swiss are sticklers for efficiency and punctuality. They, like the superb watches they manufacture, are precise. I would be disrespectful to treat them in any other manner.

The Swiss have a great deal of regard for financial know-how. Once they realize your investment decisions are sound, they will share investment strategies more openly. My relations with Swiss bankers have followed a pattern. First, the courtship — a period of time when we feel each other out, making preliminary evaluations. This time is filled with courtesies and neutral topics of conversation such as resorts, sports, and the like. Then, gingerly, we proceed into the financial area — first by covering known territory, then on to more intriguing concepts. It's like going through a series of checkpoints in a cross-country rally. Only after everything has checked out to our mutual satisfaction, with respect on both sides, do we venture into uncharted financial terrains. This process takes months, sometimes years. The Swiss can't be rushed. They are deliberate, but steady, and very astute. Many of the techniques discussed in the chapter on negotiation are applicable here. Ingratiate yourself. Fill ego and power needs — unconditional regard and confidence without arrogance. One of the most challenging and rewarding of your professional relationships will be that with your Swiss banker. His

186

ingenuity and resourcefulness are astounding. Finding the right Swiss banker is like finding a gold mine. Once you strike the mother lode, cherish your discovery!

WHERE TO LOOK

Shopping for a Swiss bank is like going to a supermarket. You have to know what you need before you buy. For the person wanting to open a small interest-bearing account in a strong currency, the so-called big-three banks are suitable. They are used to dealing with foreign clients, and are equipped to service small accounts.

They are:

Swiss Credit Bank
Paradeplatz 8
8021 Zurich, Switzerland

Union Bank of Switzerland
Bahnhofstrasse 45
8021 Zurich, Switzerland

Swiss Bank Corporation
Paradeplatz 6
8021 Zurich, Switzerland

The problem with the big three is their size. The dynamic banker you are looking for is probably there, but well insulated from the throngs of people clamoring for service. If you are dealing with larger sums of money, say $50,000 and up, you will do better to seek out the smaller private banks. This is where the true "gnomes" have hidden for years. The more money you have and the more skillful you are at negotiating, the more likely you are to rouse a financial sage from the bowels of such a bank.

For those of you who are serious treasure hunters, the following list should aptly serve as your map:

Julius Bär & Co.
Bahnhofstrasse 36
8022 Zurich, Switzerland

Lombard, Odier & Cie.
11, Rue de la Corraterie
1211 Geneva, Switzerland

Bordier & Cie.
16, rue de Hollande
1211 Geneva, Switzerland

Pictet & Cie.
6, rue Diday
1211 Geneva, Switzerland

If you do not want to manage your own investments, and if you can *clearly* convey what your investment goals are, all four of the above-listed banks will manage your funds for you on a discretionary basis. They do require minimums, however — from a $50,000 minimum at Bordier & Cie to a $300,000 minimum at the elite Julius Bär & Co. This does not mean you have to be loaded to get information and advice. These amounts apply to fully discretionary accounts only. I know one clever negotiator who wormed his way into the power structure of a highly prestigious bank with a mere $25,000. As he acquired more money, he branched out and tapped other bank sources. This silver-tongued devil is now not only flush with money, he is one of the best-educated people on international finance I have encountered. After all, he's been groomed by the world's financial elite.

CONTACTING YOUR SWISS BANK

Although you may receive contrary advice, I feel strongly that your first introduction to the Swiss banking community should be in person. Sure, you can send money off in less than $5,000 increments and get set up, but that defeats a lot of the purpose. My advice is to go there! Switzerland is one of the world's most beautiful countries. The finest skiing in the world in winter, waterfalls laden with melted snows and fields replete with wild flowers in the spring, temperate climate in the summer, and splendid color changes in the fall. You can't miss. Charming chalets nestle at the bottom of craggy cliffs. No matter which direction you choose, you will encounter shimmering, expansive lakes framed by snowcapped peaks. Combine your banking business with a vacation in Switzerland. You'll find it rewarding in many ways.

After the initial contact, you can follow up by phone. Most Swiss bankers will accept collect phone calls and charge them to your account. If you wish to protect your anonymity, use a predetermined pseudonym and call collect from a pay phone. There is no reason ever to correspond by letter. A yearly or biannual trip and interim telephone conversations should suffice.

BANK CHARGES

The cost for all this service is surprisingly small. Bank charges vary from bank to bank, and sometimes even *within* the same bank. The larger your account and the closer your relationship with your bankers, the more charges that tend to be overlooked. Swiss banks are not subject to the same scrutiny and controls as are American banks, so they enjoy more latitude in negotiating rates.

The following will provide some rough guidelines:

1) Current accounts, certificates of deposit, savings accounts, deposit accounts — no charge. The use of the client's money is sufficient compensation.

2) Foreign bonds issued in Europe — ½ percent charge in and ½ percent charge out. There is no commission charged on the purchase of new issues from your bank; the issuing company pays the commissions. This makes new-issue bonds a preferred investment vehicle and I recommend this route to perspective bond buyers.

3) Securities — On the Zurich exchange a 1-percent commission is charged on buy and sell orders. On foreign exchanges (other than Swiss) a service charge is tacked on to the standard commission. For ex-

ample, on New York Stock Exchange transactions the standard United States commission of, say, 1½ percent is charged *plus* a service charge of ½ percent to 1½ percent. For this reason it is preferable to buy stocks in United States companies on the Zurich exchange. Besides saving commission dollars, you also get to play in Swiss francs. Remember, the only difference between buying a United States-based company stock on the Swiss exchange versus the New York Stock Exchange is the factoring of the share price for currency fluctuations between the Swiss franc and the dollar. If the franc outperforms the dollar, your shares will do better on the Swiss exchange; if the dollar outperforms the franc, your Swiss shares will underperform their American counterpart. Since over the long haul odds strongly favor the franc outperforming the dollar, it pays to buy Swiss.

4) Eurocurrencies — You can buy interest-bearing currency certificates on the European market for anywhere from seven days to one year. Interest rates vary, depending on the time. Charges are ½ percent in and out plus a ten-dollar telex charge. For this reason short-term Eurocurrency investments don't pay except when large sums are involved.

5) Gold bullion — ⅜-percent commission for purchase and sale. Also an annual storage charge of 0.15 percent.

6) Gold coins — Same as for gold bullion.

7) Silver — Same as for gold bullion. Some banks charge a slightly higher storage charge (more volume for the dollar).

8) Safekeeping charges — Many banks will charge for the safekeeping of stocks and bonds. The charge is usually 0.1 percent to 0.2 percent of the net-asset value of the portfolio. Stocks are evaluated at market prices, bonds at face value. These safekeeping charges vary from bank to bank and are negotiable.

9) Managed Accounts — Discretionary accounts fully managed by the bank are tithed 0.1 percent to 0.2 percent in addition to the safekeeping charges. Again, these charges vary and are negotiable.

10) Legal advice and investment ideas — If you are clever, these pearls of international wisdom can be pried loose at no expense.

11) Referral services — Another of the pithy free services.

12) Currency exchange rates — Here again, banks have different rates for different people. They have a tourist rate, a client rate, a preferred-client rate, and a special-preferred-client rate. Naturally, when making large switches from one currency to another, the exchange rate is important. Negotiate! Here's a little tip that will save you money no matter what category you fall into — you will get more for cashier's checks or traveler's checks than you will for cash! Significantly more. Whether you are a casual traveler, an investor, or a counselor, use cashier's checks (or traveler's checks for small amounts) when transferring funds. Not only is the exchange rate better, but they are safer and less bulky. Small-denomination (less than $5,000) cashier's checks are the safest, most practical, least expensive vehicle for transferring funds to Switzerland.

FINDER'S FEES

Officially, Swiss banks will not reward persons for referring new, substantial accounts. Unofficially, they do it all the time. Sometimes they simply overlook certain periodic charges. When serious money is involved, and a finder's fee is requested as compensation, some banks will see fit to reward their benefactor and ½ percent to 1 percent of the new funds would not be out of line. The bank may want to cover itself by withholding payment for one year. This protects them from having the funds immediately withdrawn and is not an unreasonable precaution.

OTHER SERVICES

The list of possibilities involving your Swiss banker are myriad. He can make sure that financial agreements between parties are met (he will abide by any agreement between people as long as the funds to comply with the provisions are kept at the bank). He can provide contacts to many businesses and financial endeavors, refer you to accountants, lawyers, correspondents, and on and on. . . . Be creative and don't be afraid to ask. The money you save may be your own!

VI

Liechtenstein Corporations and Trusts

● Liechtenstein is a tiny principality nestled between Switzerland and Austria. Although it has only slightly more than 20,000 permanent residents, its reputation in international financial circles is vast. Virtually all of Liechtenstein's revenue comes from finance. As in Switzerland, strict bank secrecy prevails. And Liechtenstein banks have no agreements *whatsoever* with United States authorities. Although these banks are not so large or diversified as are their Swiss counterparts, they are more accommodating. Some shrewdies I know are now using Liechtenstein banks exclusively.

Besides Liechtenstein's liberal banking laws, the country has even more liberal corporate and tax laws. Several types of companies can be registered in Liechtenstein without revealing the identity of the shareholders. Shares are issued in bearer form. Whoever has them, owns them. Neither the owner's name nor that of the founder of the company is part of any public record. Liechtenstein companies owned by nonresidents pay no taxes on income earned outside of Liechtenstein. Considering that it's difficult for me to think of a way to make any money *in* Liechtenstein, this causes little concern. Strict bank secrecy, bearer shares, no taxes — sound good so far? Here are some details on how to harvest these plums.

LIECHTENSTEIN BANKS

Liechtenstein sports three (count them) banks. To my mind the best is:

Verwaltungs-und-Privat Bank
Vaduz, Liechtenstein FL-9490

This is a private bank and operates along the same lines as do Swiss private banks, with similar amenities and services. The other two banks are:

Bank in Liechtenstein, AG
(The Bank of the Prince of Liechtenstein)
Vaduz, Liechtenstein FL-9490

Liechtensteinische Landesbank
Vaduz, Liechtenstein FL-9490

The latter bank is state owned. I would avoid it since relations between Liechtenstein and the United States could impinge on privacy. "Bank in Liechtenstein" is excellent and ranks a close second to the private bank.

LIECHTENSTEIN LAWYERS

As for Liechtenstein-based companies, you first need a Liechtenstein lawyer. Fortunately, the villages are crawling with lawyers. The following is a list of reputable lawyers (or law companies) with a reputation for efficiency, accuracy, integrity, and silence:

> Allgeimeneg Treuunternehmen
> Vaduz, Liechtenstein
>
> Dr. Gerald Batliner
> Vaduz, Liechtenstein
>
> Dr. Herbert Batliner
> Vaduz, Liechtenstein
>
> Dr. Ivo Beck
> Vaduz, Liechtenstein
>
> Franz Gstöhl Consul
> Vaduz, Liechtenstein
>
> Dr. Peter Marxer
> Vaduz, Liechtenstein
>
> Praesidial Anstalt
> Vaduz, Liechtenstein

All of the above listed law-offices are established, solid, and honorable. The lawyers know their business — satisfying *your* needs — and perform it in a direct, accommodating, private manner.

Many investors combine a Swiss bank with a Liechtenstein company. Although Swiss banks can handle liquid investments for their clients with facility, nonliquid assets — such as real estate, works of art, jewelry, antiques, collections, et cetera — are unwieldy for even the most accommodating bankers. For this reason your Swiss banker may refer you to Liechtenstein. Chances are he will come up with one of the above names. If he prefers another, I would follow his advice. Your Liechtenstein representative and your Swiss banker will be working together closely, so it's best to have a happy marriage. Once you have chosen a lawyer, open up to him and tell him *all* your needs. Don't worry: it's like talking to a grave. If anyone can keep a secret better than the dead, it's the men of Liechtenstein. Their livelihood depends on it!

When your Liechtenstein lawyer has clearly understood your situation, he will recommend an appropriate corporate vehicle.

THE ESTABLISHMENT

The American press refers to all Liechtenstein companies as trusts. This is often a misnomer. Although trusts may be formed under Liechtenstein law, they are only one of several types of operating entities, and by no means the most common. The most common (and most versatile) organization is the "Establishment" (Est.). This creation, unique to Liechtenstein, exemplifies the principality's freedom and mentality. Talk about flexibility — the Establishment takes the cake! Ownership can be in the form of bearer shares or in nonshare form. An Est. can be formed by an individual, a group of individuals, a partnership, a corporation, or a trust. Liability is limited to capital; the founders and shareholders have no personal liability. Ownership may be kept absolutely secret. To do this, simply take ownership in the form of bearer shares and have these shares locked up in the vault of either a Swiss or Liechtenstein bank. The articles of incorporation are usually written in broad terms. The scope of business includes, but is not limited to, all legal and financial undertakings. This umbrella covers real estate, stocks and bonds, gold and silver bullion, commodity trading, options, works of art, antiques, collections, and numismatics. Various business endeavors such as trading companies, small businesses, large businesses, finance companies, et cetera are also covered. Your Liechtenstein Est. can be a holding company for many diversified enterprises. It can also serve as a legal vehicle for signing contracts when anonymity is desirable, and for personal services, such as property management, consulting, real-estate commissions and finders' fees.

The form of the Establishment is readily changed by merely amending the articles of incorporation. You can change it from a nonshare company to a share company, to a trust, or even to a foundation, with little difficulty.

To be in business you must meet three requirements:

1) Choose and register a name that does not conflict with the name of any other organization.
2) Elect a director who is a Liechtenstein resident.

3) Deposit 20,000 Swiss francs (SFr.) into a corporate bank account.

After you choose a name, your lawyer will register it with the state. The state does *not* know the identity of founders or shareholders. That done, it's time to elect your Liechtenstein-based director. As you stare across the highly polished burl conference table at your well-dressed, intelligent-looking lawyer, you may spark on the idea that he would make a perfect director. Besides, you're new in town and he's the only one you know. A discreet query, and Requirement Two is out of the way. All that's left is the 20,000 Swiss francs. If you already have a relationship with a Swiss bank, that's an excellent spot for the seed capital. About SFr. 7,500 go to pay the expenses of incorporation and the legal and operating expenses for the first year. And you're in business! Once established, you can withdraw the remaining funds, or use them for almost any purpose (within the limits of your articles of incorporation). Yearly maintenance runs about SFr. 4,500. For this you get full use of the abilities and facilities of your newly elected director, which includes, but is not limited to:

1) A Liechtenstein mailing address and correspondent. Your director will gladly handle all corporate correspondence, and funnel it to you in whatever circuitous manner you wish. Many people are gun-shy about receiving highly personal mail from Liechtenstein or Switzerland, so your resourceful director will arrange

for you to receive correspondence from a more neutral country, such as Austria or France.

2) A cooperative and highly efficient corporate director who can sign documents and agreements, send letters, and deposit or withdraw funds at your direction.

3) A broad shield from inquiries, either personal or governmental. Your Liechtenstein director, under penalty of law, cannot, and will not, reveal any information whatsoever about shareholders or founders. Remember the fiasco between the Swiss Credit Bank and Texon Finanzanstalt. Oh, yes, there were some distinguished Liechtenstein directors who bemoaned the tragedy of the hour, but, alas, could shed no light on the matter. Not that they had any knowledge of the hankypanky. Dishonest these directors are not. But they could not reveal any information without being guilty of a felony under Liechtenstein law, so they remained silent.

4) An extremely knowledgeable and careful confidant. Whenever a problem or question arises on how to structure a financial undertaking virtually anywhere in the world, your Liechtenstein lawyer will often have valuable input. Over the years, he has had experience with incredible varieties of financial machinations, so even your most ticklish developments are likely to be routine matters for your director. On the other hand, he will *not* volunteer advice unless asked. If you tell him to do something, he will follow out your orders without question and to your specifications. It's his job! He views it as an insult to question your judgment. So if you want his counsel, ask for it. Then, and only then, will he give you an opinion.

LIECHTENSTEIN TRUSTS

There are two basic types of trusts in Liechtenstein — the *Treuhanderschaft* and the *Treuunternehmen*. These formidable-looking German words translate into "trusteeship" and "trust undertaking" respectively. The Treuhanderschaft, like other trusts, has a designated trustee and beneficiaries. That's where the resemblance ends. The identity of the founder and all dealings of the trust may be kept secret. When secrecy is paramount, your friendly Liechtenstein lawyer takes off his director's hat and puts on his trustee's hat. The founder's identity is not recorded, so only your tight-lipped trustee is privy to the information. The trust can undertake financial dealings of every description. Its liabilities are limited to its capital. In Liechtenstein, trusts are separate entities unto themselves. The trust is not responsible for the personal financial liabilities of its founder, and as such, is untouchable by creditors of its founder. Minimum capital required to found a Treuhanderschaft is SFr. 20,000. The founder may be an individual, a corporation, a Liechtenstein Establishment, or another trust.

An acquaintance of mine who is a real bug on secrecy, decided to insulate himself against snoopers. First he established a trust under Grand Cayman Island law. In recent years the Cayman islands have made a name for themselves as a tax haven. Tight secrecy prevails, but the streets are teeming with IRS agents trying to crack the protective veil. If they are ever successful, they will find that the founder of the trust is a Liechtenstein lawyer and the beneficiary a Liechtenstein Treuhanderschaft! This cagey fellow had his Liechtenstein attorney form the Cayman Island Trust as a secrecy buffer. All financial instructions were given to the Liechtenstein lawyer, who carried them out in the name of the Grand Cayman trust. Funds were funneled through a Grand Cayman bank directly into a Swiss bank. All funds, documents, securities, et cetera wound up safely tucked away in a Swiss bank vault. If his Cayman island cover is ever cracked, the investigators will discover only the identity of the Liechtenstein founder and beneficiary — a dead end!

The Treuunternehmen is also versatile. It can be set up as a holding company, owning shares in other companies. A slight change in the articles of formation and you have a trust for a business, a corporation, an individual, or, as is usually the case, a family. Liabilities are limited to capital. As with most Liechtenstein entities, anonymity is not a problem. Minimum starting capital is SFr. 20,000.

A *Stiftung* is a foundation, as distinct from a trust. This instrument is set up to insure the execution of specific instructions on behalf of the beneficiaries. The founder may set up a Stiftung (revocable if he wishes) during his life or set up an irrevocable Stiftung as a provision of a will. If the founder desires anonymity, a Liechtenstein lawyer will gladly act as founder. A separate set of instructions, including the founder's identity and an agreement transferring founder's rights (privilege to revoke) from the Liechtenstein representative to the true founder, can be safely kept in a Swiss bank vault. The Stiftung has no owner; it is a directive, the provisions of which are faithfully executed by your Liechtenstein attorney. Minimum capital: SFr. 20,000.

If one wishes, he can form a more or less "straight" corporation under Liechtenstein law. The *Aktiengesellschaft* (AG) is a company with shares resembling these of a United States corporation. The *shares* can be held by one or more persons. The only major difference from a U.S. corporation is that bearer shares may be issued if the founders desire to screen identities. If not, shares can be registered. The AG is suitable for public offerings. Minimum capital: SFr. 50,000.

TAX CONSEQUENCE OF
LIECHTENSTEIN CORPORATIONS

As with earnings on Swiss bank accounts, profits of your Liechtenstein corporation are virtually exempt from local taxes. As for taxes in your homeland, let your conscience be your guide. United States law requires you to report income from foreign corporations, yet the identities of Liechtenstein shareholders remain an enigma. IRS inquiries are tabled by Liechtenstein lawyers in much the same fashion as obsolete articles of law are tabled by Congress. The lawyers' attitudes are of passive disinterest.

HOW TO MAINTAIN SECRECY

If secrecy is your goal, a degree of caution is desirable. The best course is not to tell anybody (save perhaps an attorney or trusted friend who is executor of your will) about your foreign corporation. The problem with secrets is that they are begging to be told. Exotic ones about Liechtenstein corporations are an overwhelming temptation for most people. They may tell only their closest friends, who tell only their closest friends, but before you know it the news has spread like fire through a parched forest.

Since you must go to Vaduz, the capital of Liechtenstein, to meet with your lawyer preparatory to setting up your corporation, establish a procedure for communications. First, pick a pseudonym. This will be your code in all contacts with your lawyer. Do not send any correspondence on your stationery; use no return addresses. It's best to contact your Liechtenstein representative by telephone or in person. Use a pay phone. Identify yourself by your chosen pseudonym. To avoid the nuisance of tens of dollars in coin at the pay phone, arrange for your lawyer to accept collect calls. Arrangements can be made to debit your Swiss or Liechtenstein bank account periodically for telephone expenses. Arrange to have mail sent from a neutral tax country, like France, Germany, or Austria. As an added precaution, you may have your Liechtenstein lawyer forward correspondence to a trustworthy United States attorney, who will then forward it to you. If you are careful, you are the only one who will know your business.

WHO SHOULD SET UP A
LIECHTENSTEIN CORPORATION

Anyone interested in pursuing financial transactions in complete privacy should consider a Liechtenstein corporation or trust. The reasons for this are myriad. Your Liechtenstein company can buy property without your creditors, friends, wife, husband, or anyone else knowing it. It can acquire works of art, rare antiques, or stock in other companies without the sellers knowing the identity of the buyer. In short, it allows you to move through the financial world invisibly, totally insulated from the hordes of drones who might otherwise seek to be your "partner."

Liechtenstein companies are not for everyone. It costs about $3,000 to set up an operating entity and about $1,200 to $1,500 for yearly maintenance. Obviously, the activities must justify the expense. This is not the province of the widow or widower with $10,000. But if your net worth is $100,000 or more, and if you seek privacy in your financial dealings, it may be worth the trouble and expense to visit quaint little Vaduz.

RELATING TO YOUR LIECHTENSTEIN LAWYER

In the race for client accommodation, it's a dead heat between Swiss bankers and Liechtenstein lawyers. The similarity in their personalities is striking. Both project an air of solidity, inspiring confidence. Neither volunteers information, but both respond knowledgeably and with alacrity to client needs and direct questions. Liechtenstein lawyers are perhaps a bit more creative than Swiss bankers. They tend to be involved in more unusual activities, since they represent company founders of every description and pursuit. Your Liechtenstein attorney has been exposed to all sorts of sophisticated financial chicanery. Your particular needs, while seeming complicated indeed to you, will probably be routine for your lawyer. Confide in him and relax. Everything will be under control.

TIMES OF INACTIVITY

If your Liechtenstein company is going to be inactive for a prolonged period of time (a year or more), special arrangements can be made with your representative. He is flexible on fee arrangements during times of inactivity. Rather than dissolve your company and set up another later, it is often better to arrange a nominal caretaking fee for your Liechtenstein lawyer and keep your existing entity alive. Then, when the time comes, you can begin again without delays. Having an intact vehicle at all times will increase your responsiveness to financial situations best handled by your Liechtenstein company. Like a checking account or credit card, your Liechtenstein operating entity may become a commonly used financial tool.

COMBINING YOUR LIECHTENSTEIN COMPANY WITH YOUR SWISS BANK

Your Liechtenstein director (lawyer, trustee, representative, correspondent) will work closely with your Swiss or Liechtenstein banker. This is standard operating procedure. He will stay in close contact so that your instructions are carried out without fail. Feel free to combine the resources of both. Agreements signed by your director that provide for incoming funds to your bank will be monitored by both parties. If your banker does not receive an expected payment, he will notify your director, who will contact you (if that has been your instruction). Whatever arrangements you set up will be executed. But remember, *execution of your orders is the sole responsibility of your agents* and they are second to none in this regard. However, if you have failed to leave complete instructions, or failed to cover all contingencies, don't expect either your banker or director to make decisions on your behalf. They just won't do it. It's best to set up an emergency procedure for them to contact you. This way, nothing is left to chance and you will eliminate slipups.

Your banker and director are formidable assets. As you gain experience in dealing with them, you will discover numerous ways in which they can be mixed and matched to best fulfill your goals.

VII

What to Do About Income Taxes

Anyone may so arrange his affairs that his taxes shall
be as low as possible; he is not bound to choose the
pattern which best pays the treasury. There is even
not a patriotic duty to increase one's taxes. Taxes are
an enforceable exaction and not a voluntary contri-
bution.

— JUDGE LEARNED HAND

● It is our duty, as citi-
zens, to pay taxes to our country. It is also our responsibility *not* to pay more than required. Each country has a
tax code governing how much tax its citizens must pay
and how such payments are computed. Responsible citizens abide by their national tax code.

In many countries of the world the payment of
taxes is a *private* matter between the citizen and his
country. They have no national tax-collection agency.
Not so in the United States. Here we have the largest,
most expensive tax-collection network in the world. Far

from being a private, moral obligation between taxpayer and country, United States tax returns are audited, probed, and investigated, and taxpayers are asked to support claims for tax reductions. The natural extension of this prying is a perpetual battle between the individual and the tax collector. The perceptive taxpayer is constantly reviewing the IRS code for loopholes in the regulations. A loophole is a provision in the IRS code, either intentional or unintentional, that provides a legitimate deduction for the aware taxpayer. Intentional loopholes are the product of special-interest-group pressures, such as the oil industry. Unintentional loopholes are oversights by the makers of the revenue code, permitting a deduction. When a loophole becomes widely used, Congress changes the law, applying putty to crevices in the code. Taxpayers and their representatives closely scrutinize the new provisions, looking for new chinks in the IRS armor. And so the game goes — the taxing authorities constantly trying to close gaps, the taxpayer looking for new ways to wriggle off the hook.

The most recent round in this fight is the 1976 Tax Reform Act. This act stitched up a lot of commonly used holes, including cattle breeding, oil exploration, financing motion pictures, and put limitations on interest deductions. Immediately the sleuths went to work. It turns out that in the crackdown on write-offs for investments in entertainment the IRS overlooked records. Record production can be financed by individuals, including the prepayment of royalties. At least this provides a shift of taxable income from one year to the next, giving the taxpayer a little breathing room and more time to arrange for more permanent tax relief. Hundreds of attorneys and accountants are currently delving into the new law, looking for other oversights. And there *will* be others. As long as only a few people discover a flaw, no changes will be made. But when a loophole becomes popular, the government cracks down, again changing the law.

REAL ESTATE

For my money, the best tax deduction, year in and year out, is real estate — the one area that remains relatively untouched during tax revisions. Private-sector investments in real estate must be encouraged. They are most important to a healthy economy. Here the government consistently gives the investor a little slack. Use it!

Income property enjoys several tax advantages. Operating costs are, of course, deductible from income. Interest, taxes, and insurance are also fully deductible. Then there is depreciation. This is the real gift. You can write off income property as if it is losing value each year. Typically, the "usable life" of a building is twenty-five years. If it depreciates the same amount every year (straight-line method), then 4 percent of the value of the structure can be deducted annually. This is a windfall. The truth of the matter is the building *appreciates* each year. It is actually going up in value while we are depreciating it for tax purposes. But to further encourage investment, the IRS has gone one step farther — accelerated depreciation. As the phrase implies, they allow the investor to depreciate a building in uneven increments, more in the early years and less later on. On a "used" building, the government will allow 125 percent accelerated depreciation. Starting with even increments of 4 percent, they will let you multiply this by 125 percent. So, instead of limiting the first-year write-off to 4 percent, it becomes 4 percent × 125 percent, or 5 percent. On new buildings they will let you go even farther; 200 percent, or so-called double declining balance, is permissible. And 4 percent × 200 percent is a whopping first-year depreciation of 8 percent! This write-off rapidly diminishes as the years pass, a hefty percentage of the depreciation being taken during the first five years. But to the taxpayer, this is pure gravy. Not only does this depreciation technique usually make whatever income the building produces *tax free*, it also reduces the tax burden from other sources. The net effect is:

1) The building throws off tax-free dollars.
2) It goes up in value.
3) The write-off from depreciation applies to other sources of income, producing more tax-free dollars.

This depreciation loophole is the cherry on the real-estate sundae. Not only is it probably the best investment on fundamentals, it also gets preferential tax treatment. How can you miss?

INDIVIDUAL CORPORATIONS

In the past five years the individual corporation has come on strong as a tax dodge. It turns out that a self-employed person may incorporate and reap the many tax loopholes currently savored by corporations. The corporation pays for all medical costs, life insurance, transportation (auto, yacht, plane), entertainment expenses (meals, club memberships, business-related travel). In short, if properly set up and administered, the "corporation" picks up the lion's share of *all* the individual's expenses. And all legal.

Corporations can also set up pension and profit-sharing plans. These plans, designed to provide for the retirement of the corporate employees, are funded with *pre-tax* dollars. Contributions are considered a direct expense to the corporation and are deducted from income before taxes are computed. Although these funds cannot be withdrawn prior to retirement, they are subject to very special tax treatment. They may be invested in a variety of ways, including savings accounts, certificates of deposit, bonds, and stocks. All income, including interest and dividends, is not taxed until the funds are dispersed to the beneficiary of the plan upon retirement, and then only at preferential capital-gain rates. The same provision applies to capital gains, both long and short term. In other words, any and all income derived from the use of these funds has tax treatment deferred for perhaps twenty to thirty years, and then is tithed at preferred rates! If there happens to be only one employee in this corporation, so be it. That employee is entitled to *all* the corporate benefits, including his very own pension and profit-sharing plan. Each year 25 percent of his salary, up to a maximum of $25,000 annually, may be tucked away in his pension and profit-sharing plan. When you combine this with the unheard-of luxury of deferring taxes on all income, these plans can quickly swell into burgeoning fortunes!

But what a waste! There you sit with all that loot, and you can't lay a pinkie on it until you're sixty-five. Here you are, a successful forty-five-year-old engineer with $200,000 stashed away in your own personal pension and profit-sharing plan, and you must wait another *twenty years* before receiving even a nosegay. Enter the loophole! The law provides that pension and profit-sharing plans can make loans to credit-worthy parties. Who do you know who is more credit-worthy than yourself? Besides, for once you have an inside track to the money. You provide the plan with the usual financial statement and loan documents, make healthy interest payments (after all, the loan is unsecured), and the plan lends you somewhat familiar money. What do you do with it? You turn around and buy real estate. Income-producing property. More tax-free income. More depreciation to shelter more of your other income. You must, of course, pay interest to your plan, at, say, 10 percent. This interest is tax-deferred for the plan. But you, as an individual, are entitled to deduct the 10 percent you pay *now* against your current income. Pay interest to yourself and get a deduction? Absolutely! Another loophole.

As time goes on you repay your plan in full, then borrow again, more this time. Can you see the synergy? You are well on your way to setting up a situation that will mushroom into vast personal holdings with minimal tax consequences. The individual corporation is a nonstop ticket to wealth.

DEFINED BENEFIT PLANS

As we have seen, in the tax game the mouse is always trying to stay a step ahead of the cat. A clever actuary came up with a scheme to squeeze more income into a retirement plan than the standard 25 percent ($25,000 maximum). He set it up, bounced it off the IRS, and, lo and behold, it flew! The result was the defined-benefit pension plan. Currently, you can fund your pension plan to guarantee a maximum income upon retirement of $84,500 annually. The standard used to provide for this income is an annuity yielding the yearly $84,500.

An annuity is a vehicle issued by an insurance company. A lump sum of money is given to the insurance company, then they guarantee yearly income payments for the rest of the buyer's life. Different insurance companies issue different annuities. For the purpose of funding a defined-benefit pension plan, the *worst* annuity available is selected as a standard. The reason the worst annuity is selected is because the individual funding his pension plan wants to stuff as much money as possible in his plan in as short a time as he can. The worse the annuity, the more money required to yield the desired $84,500. In actuality, the creator of the pension plan has no intention of using an annuity to provide income at retirement. As an investment, annuities, like ordinary life insurance, rank right behind flushing your money down the toilet. But for establishing the amounts needed to fund a defined-benefit retirement plan, they are unequaled. Besides, the IRS recognizes them as acceptable criteria for funding. So be it.

To assure $84,000 on retirement requires the accumulation, over the years, of $1,250,000 to $1,500,000 in the pension plan. Now the actuary goes to work. He takes your current age and calculates how much you need to fund your pension plan each year to accumulate the necessary funds to buy the annuity. The closer you are to retirement, the more funds you can chunk away each year, avoiding taxes. Some high-salaried professionals I know who incorporated late are socking away $100,000 a year in their defined-benefit plan. Remember, this funding is a straight deduction from earned income!

Younger guys (and gals) cannot put away as much each year as their older compatriots. But they can come close, thanks to guess what? The ever-present loophole. The argument revolves around what is an appropriate age to retire. Most pension plans are based on sixty-five as the age of retirement. Exceptions are extended only to areas where the industry practice is earlier retirement, such as hazard-prone industries. A while back a neurosurgeon claimed "industry practice" was to retire at age fifty-five. He funded his retirement plan accordingly and the plan was approved by the IRS. That opened up the floodgates. Next, *all* surgeons claimed early retirement at fifty-five. Then all doctors. In February of 1976 the IRS threw in the sponge. They decided not to question retirement age in pension plans as long as it was set at fifty-five or more. This was the break younger, high-income earners were waiting for. Instead of $25,000 a year, this opening allows them to fund their defined-benefit plan with $40,000 to $60,000, depending on age and setup for the plan. A good actuary will tell you how to do it. There are actuaries who now do nothing but set up pension plans for one-employee corporations. This is the kind of talent you want when you are dealing with this fluid field. There are still many areas that are up in the air, and the rules of the game are constantly changing, so there is no substitute for top-flight professional help.

INCOME-TAX TREATIES

Citizens of foreign countries not residing in the United States (nonresident aliens) may make investments or conduct business in the United States. So may foreign corporations and trusts.

A foreign citizen or corporation investing in the United States would potentially have a dual tax liability — a United States obligation and an obligation at home. To get around this double-taxation issue, the United States has negotiated "tax treaties" with twenty-seven nations. It is not within the purview of this book to describe in detail the myriad, complicated gyrations of international tax treaties. This is the province of the tax attorney, a highly specialized lawyer. If you are going to get your feet wet in this area, I suggest you find a competent tax attorney. Consult your personal attorney or your local Bar Association.

To give you an idea of how tax treaties work and some of the possible spin-offs, let's have a look at interest. Interest is capital earned on loaned funds. The United States generally withholds 30 percent of all interest earned in the United States by nonresident aliens.

Of the tax-treaty countries this same 30 percent with-holding applies to Australia, Italy, New Zealand, Pakistan, South Africa, Trinidad and Tobago, and the Union of Soviet Socialist Republics.

Under certain conditions the following countries are entitled to reductions in the United States withholding rate:

1) Belgium 15 percent
2) Canada 15 percent
3) France 10 percent
4) Japan 10 percent
5) Rumania 10 percent
6) Switzerland 5 percent
7) Austria — exempt
8) Denmark — exempt
9) Finland — exempt
10) Germany — exempt
11) Greece — exempt
12) Iceland — exempt
13) Ireland — exempt
14) Luxembourg — exempt
15) Netherlands — exempt
16) Netherlands Antilles — exempt
17) Norway — exempt
18) Poland — exempt
19) Sweden — exempt
20) The United Kingdom — exempt

The conditions under which this reduced withholding prevails vary from country to country. In some countries it applies only to interest received by an individual. Interest received by a holding company may not be entitled to the exemption (Luxembourg). Some countries exclude mortgage interest from the exemption, and so on. Your tax attorney will have all the details.

These treaties are of obvious benefit to foreign nationals, but they also have implications for the United States citizen not averse to going to some trouble to avoid taxes. A lady I know decided some years back that it would be prudent to stash a little loot in a Swiss bank.

She wrestled with the moral issue of reporting her decision to the United States tax authorities on her yearly income-tax statements. She decided on a compromise that would cover all bases. She opened *two* accounts at the same bank. One account was in her name; she seeded it with a few thousand dollars. The second account was a numbered account that she funded with a far larger sum. She proceeded to check "yes" to the question on her tax return about foreign bank accounts. Predictably, the return was tagged and a revenue agent queried her. She freely admitted to having a Swiss bank account and cooperatively showed the agent full records of the smaller account. Case closed. The larger account escaped unnoticed, as the agent neglected to ask her if she had any other accounts. She had answered all statements and questions frankly, although not volunteering additional information.

She made several trips to check on her money and established a particularly close relationship with a high-ranking bank officer. Months later opportunity knocked. She had a chance to write a second mortgage on a piece of property with an effective yield of 12 percent *and* a healthy share of the profits upon sale. She consulted a tax attorney and learned that Swiss citizens and corporations are covered by a tax treaty. Interest, including mortgage interest, is subject to withholding of only 5 percent. The banker was kind enough to advance the funds in his name, debiting her account, and covering their arrangement with a signed agreement tucked away in the bank vault. The net effect is that she received all the benefits (less 5 percent of the interest received, 11.4 percent net) plus a capital gain down the line.

I want to make it clear that I do not condemn or condone this kind of financial manipulation. I'm only pointing out what some people are doing in reaction to what they view as a frank invasion of privacy on the part of national tax agencies. Most of these ploys are cleverly concealed and are unlikely to be discovered.

The most extreme example of using tax loopholes to the fullest is the case of the famed California tax attorney, Mr. Margolis. He carefully dissected the revenue codes, especially the rulings related to foreign tax havens and offshore trusts. He was subjected to a full-scale investigation that resulted in a series of indictments. After several years of legal battles at tremendous expense to both his time and resources, he was acquitted on all counts of tax evasion. He claimed all along that he didn't make the laws, he only used what the law provided, giving his clients the best possible tax-saving advice under the existing statutes.

FUTURE TAX LEGISLATION

At the time of this writing, President Carter is taking a hard look at the tax situation preparatory to making definitive recommendations to Congress on a tax-reform package. Although a wide range of ideas is being bandied about, certain provisions have a high probability of being part of the final package.

Preferential treatment of capital gains may be eliminated. This would modestly dampen investment enthusiasm and would be imprudent in my opinion.

A much greater threat to investors is the proposed limitation on the amount of interest expense that can be deducted. One proposal includes limiting to $10,000 total annual interest that can be written off. Another limits investment-interest deductions to $10,000 and mortgage-interest deductions to $10,000. The latter program is restrictive, the former impossible. If either of these proposals becomes reality, personal investment incentives will be choked off. Strong lobbying efforts are being made by banks, savings and loans, mortgage finance companies, and brokerage houses to prevent these limitations.

The other side of the ledger includes initiatives for some tax relief on dividend payments and an increase in the investment-tax credit to promote capital expenditures by business.

Other proposals cover a gamut of issues, including the elimination of accelerated depreciation on real estate, and a minimum tax to be paid by all.

What the eventual outcome of all this will be is pure conjecture. It seems clear, however, that personal investment incentives are going to be curtailed to a greater or lesser extent. Once again the sleuths will have to be called in to unearth oversights and make interpretations in the new code. And the wheel turns.

There appears to be no end in sight to this parrying between taxpayer and tax collector. It seems to me that a better solution might be a fixed tax on income — say 20 percent to 25 percent for *everyone,* rich or poor. This would provide the government with needed revenues and cut through all the muck that currently exists.

What would be saved by eliminating the current expensive tax bureaucracy would foot the bill for a large part of the welfare program. But short of this, the game will continue, and, as with all games, the best players will win.

EPILOGUE

If this book leaves you with no other thought, let it be this: it is unnecessary to regard making money as a cold, cut-throat activity. You need not alienate others in the process of fulfilling your needs. By understanding the game you are playing and effectively utilizing your own resources, you will be successful. Positive human interaction is the secret to making money.

GLOSSARY

The following is a glossary of terms used in the stock-market chapter. These terms are defined *as used in the context of this chapter,* and are not necessarily *general* definitions for these terms.

ANNUALIZED RETURN — The return on an investment factored for a one-year period. A 6-percent return in three months is an *annualized return* of 24 percent.

ASKED PRICE — The price being *asked* by persons wanting to sell a security.

BACK OFFICE — The clerical departments of a brokerage house: accounting, posting, shipping and receiving, et cetera.

BEAR MARKET — A prolonged downward trend in the stock market.

"BELLWETHER" STOCKS — Representative stocks of different industry groups that I follow as a guideline. See Table II, pp. 71–73.

BID PRICE — The price being offered by persons wanting to buy a security.

BOND — A long-term corporate debt. A company borrows money from individuals and institutions, promising to repay the borrowed amount at a specified time and at a fixed rate of interest.

BROKER — A licensed security salesman.

BROKERAGE HOUSE — A company whose business is buying and selling securities, arranging financing for corporations, and investment banking.

BULL MARKET — A prolonged upward trend in the stock market.

"BULLPEN" — In many brokerage houses the junior brokers do not have private offices. They sit in a big room filled with many desks. This room is called the *bullpen.*

BUY SIGNAL — A specialist short-sale ratio of 40 percent or less and a NYSE member short-sale ratio of 65 percent or less.

CALL OPTION — The right to buy a security at a given price for a specified period of time, e.g.: *Tandy, Jan. 22, 1977, 40* is the right to buy 1 share of Tandy Corp. at $40 dollars per share at any time up until Jan. 22, 1977.

COMPOUND-GROWTH RATE — The growth of a company including growth of the expanded revenues, e.g.: at 15 percent compound growth rate on $1,000,000 is $1,150,000 the first year; $1,322,500 the second year; $1,520,875 the third year. . . .

CONVERTIBLE BOND — A corporate debt, like a regular bond, but with an added proviso that the owner can *convert* his loan into an equivalent dollar amount of common stock, at a specified price, at any time until maturity.

COVERED OPTION — When the writer of a call option simultaneously purchases an equal number of shares of the underlying stock.

CUMULATIVE GROSS COMMISSION OR "CUM. GROSS" — The sum of the gross commissions accumulated by a broker.

DEBT — A corporate financial obligation.

DELIVERY-VERSUS-PAYMENT — Payment for securities when the actual physical certificate is delivered by the brokerage house to the buyer.

DIVIDEND — A distribution of a portion of the profits to shareholders of a company.

DOW, DJIA — Dow Jones Industrial Average.

DRAFT — A written demand for payment of a security accompanying the certificates when a stock is delivered versus payment.

DUE BILL — An obligation.

ECONOMIC CYCLE — Changing economic conditions and variables that repeat themselves in a predictable pattern.

ECONOMIC PAUSE — A plateau in a long-term economic growth curve; a temporary lull in a period of economic growth.

EQUITIES — Stocks.

EXECUTION — The carrying out of an order to buy or sell a security.

FED — The Federal Reserve Board, an independent organization set up to exercise fiscal controls in the United States.

FIXED-INCOME SECURITIES — Securities with a rate of return that does not change.

FLOAT — That period of time between purchase of an interest-bearing security and delivery of that security to a bank for payment, when interest is accruing without funds having been advanced.

FOUR-WEEK MOVING AVERAGE — The average of a group of four weekly figures. As each new week is added, the oldest week's figure is deleted.

GROSS COMMISSION — The overall commission paid by a client to a brokerage firm.

GROUP ROTATION — The upward or downward movement of the stock of certain industries that coincides with different parts of the economic cycle.

"HOT" NEW ISSUE — A new public offering where demand far exceeds supply, and where the shares immediately appreciate when released on the open market.

INITIAL PUBLIC OFFERING — The first offering to the public of shares in a company.

INSTITUTIONS — Large organizations which commonly buy or sell securities, including mutual funds, banks, and insurance companies.

INSTITUTIONAL DEPARTMENT — A division within a brokerage house specifically designed to cater to institutions.

INTERNATIONAL HERALD TRIBUNE — A widely circulated international newspaper, in English, containing current security quotations.

LEVERAGE — Increasing purchasing power for securities. Usually accomplished by borrowing funds from either a bank or a brokerage house.

LIQUIDITY — In cash, or *readily* convertible into cash.

LONG POSITION — Owning a security that has not yet

been delivered or is being held in safekeeping. Going long is the same as buying.

MARGIN — Borrowing money from a brokerage house for the purchase of securities, using the security as collateral for the loan.

MARGIN INTEREST RATE — The amount of interest a brokerage house charges a client on his margin account.

MARKET CORRECTION — A temporary downward phase in a stock market when the primary trend is upward (bullish).

MONEY SUPPLY — The amount of money in public hands.

MOODY'S CORPORATE BOND INDICATOR — A compilation by Moody's rating service of the average price of various bonds. A useful broad index of current bond-interest rates.

NAKED OPTION — Writing a call option on a stock *without* owning the underlying stock.

NEUTRAL BAND OF INDICATOR — The range of the specialist short-sales indicator between 40 and 60 percent and member short-sales indicator between 65–75 percent.

NEW ISSUE — The marketing of a security previously unavailable to the public.

NEW ISSUE CALENDAR — A schedule of forthcoming securities issues with probable release dates.

NINETY-DAY TREASURY-BILL YIELD — The return on investment on Treasury bills due in ninety days.

NYSE — New York Stock Exchange.

OFFERING PRICE — The price at which a new issue or secondary issue is offered to the public.

OPEN MARKET ORDER — An order to buy or sell a security on one of the exchanges, or over the counter, at prevailing market prices.

OPTION PREMIUM — A non-refundable amount of money paid by the buyer of an option to the person who writes (offers) the option.

OTC — Abbreviation for over-the-counter market.

OUTSTANDING SHARES — The number of shares of a company that have been issued to shareholders.

OVERSUBSCRIBED — Orders for a new issue in excess of the number of shares available for purchase.

P/E RATIO — Abbreviation for price/earnings ratio: The market price of a stock divided by the annual earnings of that company.

PRIMARY TREND — The basic direction of the stock or bond market, either up or down.

PROFIT-LOSS COLUMN — A column in my journal where I record the profit, or loss, on each completed security transaction.

"QUID PRO QUO" — Latin term which, loosely translated, means "value for value received."

SEC — Abbreviation for Securities and Exchange Commission; the regulatory body that controls the securities' industry.

SECONDARY ISSUE — The release of additional stock by a company whose shares are already available to the public.

SELL SIGNAL — When the specialist short-sale indicator is 60 percent or higher and member short-sale indicator is 80 percent or more.

SHORT SALE — The sale of a stock without prior ownership. The shares are "borrowed" from a brokerage house, then returned when the short sale is covered (shares are bought); reversal of the normal process: selling first and buying later. The short seller is betting that the stock will go *down*.

S & P — Abbreviation for Standard & Poor's; a rating-service and financial-service company.

SPECIALIST — An individual on the floor of a security exchange who makes a market in one or more securities.

SPECIALIST SHORT SALES — The amount of shares shorted by the specialists as a group over a given time period, in this case one week.

SPECIALIST SHORT-SALE INDICATOR — The percentage of short selling being done by the specialist in one week.

SPECIALIST SHORT-SALE RATIO — Specialist short sales divided by total short sales in a one-week period.

STANDARD & POOR'S 400 INDUSTRIAL AVERAGE — A compilation of prices of 400 industrial stocks. A good, broad-based indicator of stock prices.

STOCK-MARKET CYCLE — A repetitive pattern of movement, up and down, of stock prices.

STOCK PORTFOLIO — The total stock holdings of an individual or institution.

STRIKING PRICE — The agreed-upon price where a stock may be purchased under an option contract at any time until expiration of the option.

SYNDICATE — A group of brokers formed for the orderly marketing of a new issue or secondary.

T-BILL INDICATOR — A change in the 10-month moving average of 90-day Treasury-bill yields, in the same direction, either up or down, for 3 consecutive months.

TECHNICAL SUPPORT — As used here, a service predicting probable stock-market movement, either up or down, by analyzing variables such as volume, advance-decline lines, up-down volume, and many other technical charts and graphs.

TEN-MONTH MOVING AVERAGE — The average of a group of 10 monthly figures. As each new month is added, the oldest month's figure is deleted.

TOTAL SHORT SALES — Cumulative sum of *all* short sales over a one-week period.

UNDERWRITING — An agreement between a brokerage house, or a group of brokerage houses, and a company, to market a security offering of that company.

YIELD — Percentage return on investment.

YIELD SPREAD — The difference between the percentage returns on investment of bonds and stocks.